STRATEGIC
READINESS

John C. Redding
Ralph F. Catalanello

STRATEGIC READINESS

The Making of the Learning Organization

Jossey-Bass Publishers
San Francisco

Substantial discounts on bulk quantities of Jossey-Bass books are available to corporations, professional associations, and other organizations. For details and discount information, contact the special sales department at Jossey-Bass Inc., Publishers. (415) 433-1740; Fax (415) 433-0499.

For sales outside the United States, contact Maxwell Macmillan International Publishing Group, 866 Third Avenue, New York, New York 10022.

Manufactured in the United States of America. Nearly all Jossey-Bass books and jackets are printed on recycled paper containing at least 10 percent postconsumer waste, and many are printed with either soy- or vegetable-based ink, which emits fewer volatile organic compounds during the printing process than petroleum-based ink.

Library of Congress Cataloging-in-Publication Data

Redding, John C., date.
  Strategic readiness : the making of the learning organization / John C. Redding, Ralph F. Catalanello. — 1st ed.
      p.   cm. — (The Jossey-Bass management series)
  Includes bibliographical references and index.
  ISBN 1-55542-633-6
    1. Organizational change—Management.   2. Preparedness.
3. Learning.   I. Catalanello, Ralph F., date.   II. Title.
III. Series.
HD58.8.R377   1994
658.4'06—dc20   93-48673
                                                                      CIP

Credits are on pp. 201–202.

FIRST EDITION
HB Printing   10 9 8 7 6 5 4 3 2 1   *Code 9430*

The Jossey-Bass Management Series

Consulting Editors
Human Resources

Leonard Nadler
Zeace Nadler
College Park, Maryland

CONTENTS

PREFACE

Strategic Readiness is about a significant idea with far-reaching implications: most organizational change results not from formal plans and fixed programs for change but from a process of learning—and not just from the learning of individuals but, more importantly, from the collective learning of entire organizations.

Firms that aggressively and systematically work to develop their learning capacity, and therefore their ability to continuously adapt and transform themselves, are what we call learning organizations.

Much is being written today about learning organizations. But the notion that organizations have the capacity to learn has actually been around for quite some time. Pioneers in the study of the subject include Chris Argyris, Reg Revans, Donald Schön, and Herbert Simon. In the mid 1970s, Royal Dutch/Shell made an important contribution to the concept of the learning organization with its recognition of learning as the central component of strategic change and competitive survival (de Geus, 1988). Moreover, the quality improvement movement of recent years, with its emphasis on *continuous* improvement, has been recognized as the first broad (if incomplete) application of learning organization concepts (Senge, 1991).

The current interest in learning organizations was ignited by the publication of Peter Senge's *The Fifth Discipline* (1990). But even before *The Fifth Discipline* was published, *Fortune* magazine observed that the notion of the learning organization was becoming "a very big conceptual catchall to help us make sense of a set of values and ideas we've been wrestling with, everything from customer service to corporate responsiveness and speed" (Kiechel, 1990, p. 133).

Purpose of the Book

What does *Strategic Readiness* bring to the discussion? It adds perspective in two key ways. First, its main focus is not individual learning or team learning but the organization-wide process through which entire firms plan, implement, and modify strategic directions. Second, it attempts to move beyond abstract descriptions of learning organizations and offers numerous concrete illustrations of learning organizations in action.

Background

With this book, as with most successful change efforts in organizations, original intention and final accomplishment, in retrospect, appear almost unrelated. The wide gulf that separates the two represents a journey of learning: the greater the gap, the greater the journey. Considerable learning occurred in the writing of this book.

Our personal journeys of learning about organizational change started many years ago. Early in our careers, we were each involved in highly promising but ultimately ill-fated strategic change efforts. For one of us, it was launching an exciting participative management experiment in a core division of a major manufacturing corporation. For the other, it was introducing an innovative system that had the potential to revolutionize the administration of rural health care. Early enthusiasm and successes gave way, in both cases, to broad-based resistance and, ultimately, failure. These were defining experiences for each of us. In many ways, our subsequent careers have been spent attempting to explain why well-intentioned, well-planned, and fully supported change efforts are so often unsuccessful.

Our approach to writing the book was as follows: we first

conducted a research study of approximately two hundred organizations. These included several firms, such as Micro Switch and Motorola, that are featured in the book, as well as others that are not—Apple Computer, General Dynamics, and Servicemaster among them. We sought to determine why certain organizations were more successful at change than others.

The results of the study surprised us. The quality of strategic plans did not seem to have much to do with companies' ability (or lack of ability) to change. Nor did the degree of effort devoted to the implementation of strategic plans seem to explain the difference. Instead, what seemed to matter most was the organization's readiness for change—a concept we now call strategic readiness.

In addition, we examined a growing body of research that indicated that strategic change occurred through a process of organizational experimentation and learning (Beer, Eisenstat, and Spector, 1990; de Geus, 1988).

Next, we developed in-depth case studies of several organizations actively applying learning organization concepts. In many cases, especially if the reader picks up and reads just a section of *Strategic Readiness*, it may seem that many of the practical applications described here represent nothing new. Ambitious employee communication programs, experimental approaches to strategy implementation, conflict management, temporary organizational structures, shared vision—none of these is a novel idea. What is different about these case studies is the intensity, intent, and scope of the efforts of these learning organizations. No longer are these activities isolated events; they are components of systemic interventions designed to increase the learning capacity of organizations. These efforts show that, in terms of learning, the whole is truly more than the sum of its parts.

Audience

Strategic Readiness is primarily written for those currently involved in significant change in their organizations. As such, it is directed to those in middle- and upper-level management positions who are responsible for making change happen. But everyone who is a member of an organization is involved in change, and this book is relevant for any person who wants to obtain a better understanding of the intricacies of organizational learning and transformation. Consultants should find this book helpful in their learning organization interventions and will be able to use it as a tool for educating clients. Academics should discover that the book is a useful supplementary text for courses in organization theory, strategic management, organization behavior, organization development, and human resource development.

Overview of the Contents

The book starts with a prologue, which provides an overview of organizational learning as a comprehensive approach to planning and implementing strategic change. It is essentially an overture, sounding the major themes developed throughout the remainder of the book.

The core of the book consists of nine chapters divided into three parts, each part three chapters long. The first three chapters make up Part One. Chapter One examines the parallels between individual and organizational learning processes; how individuals learn from their daily experiences can illuminate how organizations learn as they plan, implement, and modify business strategies. Chapter Two shows how learning organizations try to increase the speed, extend the depth, and widen the breadth of their strategic learning. Chapter Three explores the importance of building the readiness of the organization to learn.

The next three chapters, which make up Part Two, offer concrete examples of the steps leading organizations are taking to accelerate strategic learning through continuous planning (Chapter Four), improvised implementation (Chapter Five), and deep reflection (Chapter Six).

Chapters Seven through Nine form Part Three, which offers illustrations of ways an organization can prepare to learn by heightening its awareness of the need for change (Chapter Seven), making learning a way of life (Chapter Eight), and becoming a continuously self-organizing system (Chapter Nine).

The book concludes with an epilogue, which uses jazz improvisation as an analogy to highlight and summarize the defining

characteristics of learning organizations as described throughout
the book.

Acknowledgments

Our thanks are many: to Leonard Nadler and Zeace Nadler, who
first approached us with the idea that led to this book; to the many
people who shared their organizations' stories with us, including
Ray Alvarez, Susan Berryman, Tom Broersma, Mark Cheren, Steve
Goldman, Alan Honeycutt, Deborah Lauer, Steve Lichter, Kay Ri-
ley, and Paul Woolner; to Linda Morris, John Niemi, Muriel
Niemi, and Elaine Winter, who supplied valuable guidance on
early manuscripts; to Bill Hicks and Cedric Crocker of Jossey-Bass
Publishers, who have served not only as editors but also as colleagues and collaborators; and to Mary Garrett for a superb job of
managing the production of the book.

Our final thanks go to those who really made this book possible—our wives and families. To Kathy and to Mary Ann and Jody,
Mark, and Peter: you provided the support and encouragement to
help us see this project through.

January 1994   JOHN C. REDDING
                                                  Naperville, Illinois

                                                  RALPH F. CATALANELLO
                                                  DeKalb, Illinois

THE AUTHORS

John C. Redding is a management consultant specializing in organizational learning and strategic change. He also serves as adjunct professor at Northern Illinois University, designing and leading graduate workshops on the learning organization and strategic human resource development. Redding has served as a consultant to such firms as Borg-Warner, Motorola, and Official Airline Guides. He has also served as director of training and organization development for Geo. J. Ball, Inc./Ball Seed Company, a leading international horticultural corporation.

Redding received his Ph.D. degree (1990) from Northern Illinois University in adult learning and strategic management. His dissertation, "An Analysis of Three Strategic Training Roles: Their Impact upon Strategic Planning Problems," received the American Society for Training and Development Donald Bullock Dissertation of the Year Award. He is a frequent presenter at national conferences and has authored numerous articles on strategy, learning, and change.

Ralph F. Catalanello is professor of management at Northern Illinois University. He received his Ph.D. degree (1971) from the University of Wisconsin in management and organization. He has taught courses in strategic management, international management, and organization design, and he has presented more than fifty papers at national and international conferences.

Catalanello has extensive national and international consulting experience in strategic human resource planning and development, working with such organizations as NASA's Johnson Space Center, Manor Care, and Sundstrand. He is author of numerous articles, some of which have appeared in the *Training and Development Journal,* the *Human Resource Planning Journal, Personnel,* and the *Personnel Administrator.* He is a member of the Academy of Management, the Academy of International Business, the Association for Business Simulation and Experiential Learning, and the Society for the Advancement of Management.

STRATEGIC
READINESS

Prologue

The Call for Learning Organizations

Noah's principle: one survives not by predicting rain
but by building arks.

Once seemingly calm and tranquil, business environments are becoming increasingly uncertain and turbulent. Swirling gusts of technological, competitive, political, and marketplace changes are sweeping across the global business landscape. Amid these uncertain conditions, many leading firms are constructing arks comprising their collective capacity to learn—not just as individuals, but as entire organizations. In other words, they are striving to become *learning organizations.*

One such organization is Royal Dutch/Shell. In a milestone article published in 1988, Arie de Geus, head of planning for Royal Dutch/Shell, asserted that successful strategic planning—strategic planning that ensures that firms survive from one period in their history to another, even when competitors do not—can best be thought of as a process of learning, not just of individuals but of entire organizations.

Surviving the Storm: The Royal Dutch/Shell Story

Few industries have been more uncertain than the international petroleum industry in which Royal Dutch/Shell has thrived for over one hundred years. In the oil business, the cost of raw materials can jump ten times from one day to the next. Uncontrollable international crises can turn the gas pump on or off and open or close markets in a few days. And at any time, accidental spills and other accidents can cost over $3 billion a shot.

Hoping to discover ways to ensure its own survival, Shell conducted a study of thirty companies that had survived more than seventy-five years (compared to the average of about forty years). The study concluded that these firms persevered because of their capacities "to absorb what is going on in the business environment and to act on that information with appropriate business moves. In other words, [their survivals] depend[ed] on learning. Or more precisely, on institutional learning, which is the process whereby management teams change their shared mental models of their company, their markets, and their competitors. For this reason, we think of planning as learning and of corporate planning as institutional learning" (de Geus, 1988, p. 70).

Over the past two decades, Shell has instituted an aggressive series of steps to transform its ability to learn into a competitive weapon:

- While its chief competitors, such as the giant Exxon Corporation, have become increasingly centralized, Shell has systematically given more and more autonomy to its 260 operating divisions, promoting quick action and experimentation.
- Shell has developed "war games" to ready the crews of its 114 tankers for unexpected breaks in oil supply. As a result, Chairman Lodewijk van Wachem reports that during the 1991 Persian Gulf war, "I don't think we missed a beat" (Knowlton, 1991, p. 82).
- Shell has pioneered the use of scenario planning. Recognizing that it is unable to forecast the future, Shell develops detailed scenarios of several different possible futures and develops strategies that maximize Shell's success across the range of differing scenarios.
- Shell has implemented the "management challenge," a process by which peer managers question the assumptions underlying each others' business plans and operations.

- *Shell consciously keeps things shaken up by changing the rules—such as when and how planning is done—to break up the old "corporate rain dance" and to promote new ways of thinking.*
- *Shell uses computer-based models to simulate the future impact of actions so managers can "learn from their experience" before they actually have it.*

According to available evidence, Royal Dutch/Shell's approach to viewing "planning as learning" seems to be working. In 1990, Shell surpassed Exxon in total revenues and became the world's largest oil company, with only General Motors ahead of it on the Global 500 list of the largest industrial corporations. Moreover, from 1972 to 1992, Shell stock rose from twelfth to fourth in market value of all companies worldwide.[1]

Royal Dutch/Shell is ambitiously striving to transform itself into a *learning organization*. But what exactly is a learning organization? David Garvin of the Harvard Business School offers the following definition: "A learning organization is an organization skilled at creating, acquiring, and transferring knowledge, and at modifying its behavior to reflect new knowledge and insights" (1993, p. 80).

According to Garvin, to be considered a learning organization, a firm must build its capacity both to *think* in new ways and to *act* based upon the new knowledge.

The initially intriguing concept of learning organizations can quickly dissipate into a vague abstraction. Contributing to the problem is the common use of such obscure terminology as paradigms, mind-sets, mental models, double-loop learning, systems thinking, and neural networks. We agree with Tom Peters: "Most talk about 'learning organizations' is maddingly abstract or vague— and perpetually falls short on the specifics" (1992, p. 385). It is our primary purpose in this book to get specific about learning organizations. In the next nine chapters, we tell the story of several firms striving to become learning organizations, including:

• *TRW Space and Defense Group.* In the mid 1980s no one could predict the dramatic events soon to occur in the Soviet Union and Eastern Europe. Yet TRW Space and Defense Group, a leading manufacturer of "spy" satellites, began its first steps toward transforming itself into a learning organization capable of changing faster than its environment. It looked to find ways in which its technologies and expertise could be deployed across a wide range of different applications, some for the defense industry, many not. It set up systems through which information would be rapidly spread throughout the firm. The results? When defense industry contracts dissipated a few years later, TRW was one of the very few corporations in the defense and aerospace industry not to have layoffs, moving into new and different businesses faster than the competition.[2]

• *Honeywell Micro Switch.* A few years ago, Ray Alvarez took over responsibility for Honeywell's Micro Switch division, a leading diversified electronics producer. A dominant player in its industry for many years, Micro Switch had, from Alvarez's perspective, become complacent. Although problems loomed on the horizon (including declining profitability, increasingly aggressive competition, and rising customer dissatisfaction), few seemed to notice. Alvarez's early suggestions that fundamental change was needed met widespread resistance. In fact, many managers were convinced that the company had a good shot at winning the prestigious Malcolm Baldrige National Quality Award.

Alvarez quickly realized that for the company to change it would have to become ready to change. So, Alvarez's first job was to help the company generate a sense of healthy dissatisfaction with the status quo and appreciate the necessity for continuous change. He encouraged the management team to submit a Baldrige Award application to obtain clear feedback on how far the company had to go to achieve world-class standards of quality improvement. In addition, he launched an ambitious series of steps to keep people informed of customer needs, competitor moves, and marketplace trends. Finally, he worked with the management team to challenge and reward people—both as individuals and in groups—for increasing contributions to performance excellence. As of today, Micro Switch has still not won the Baldrige Award, but it has been recognized as the number one supplier by several top customers. But even more important, according to Alvarez, Micro Switch now appreciates the necessity of becoming "a learning organization, relentlessly pursuing new knowledge, and applying the new knowledge in the pursuit of continuous improvement."[3]

- *Motorola.* This Baldrige Award–winning electronics manufacturer is approaching a milestone, the achievement of "six sigma," a previously unheard-of level of defects: less than 3.4 per million opportunities for errors. Yet it took the company approximately fourteen years to achieve this objective. Recently, the company studied six sigma as a process of organizational learning, noting key milestones, breakthroughs, and roadblocks. With this new understanding, it has set the goal of reducing the duration of its corporation-wide learning process by one-half (from fourteen to seven years) with its new strategic initiative of becoming a leader in integrating hardware and software.[4]

Royal Dutch/Shell, TRW Space and Defense, Honeywell Micro Switch, and Motorola are all aspiring to become learning organizations. But a word of caution: to simply copy these techniques and methods, as well as those of others featured later in the book, would be a mistake. There is no blueprint of the ideal learning organization. In fact, what distinguishes these firms is their recognition that they must discover their *own* solutions rather than borrow them. They accept that the answers to their most pressing strategic problems will not come neatly wrapped in a box, whether that box be labeled "the definitive strategic business plan," "the latest management panacea," or even "the best practices of the most successful companies."

What, then, do learning organizations have in common?

- They continuously experiment rather than search for final solutions.
- They respect improvisation more than forecasts.
- They devise new actions rather than defend past actions.
- They cultivate impermanence rather than permanence.
- They strive for argument rather than serenity.
- They encourage doubt rather than remove it.
- They seek contradictions rather than discourage them.[5]

Most significantly, learning organizations recognize that successful strategic change is best approached as *journeys of learning*.

Journeys of Learning

What do we mean by journeys of learning? An analogy may help. Picture yourself taking a trip into the Rocky Mountains. As you set out and look toward the mountains, the hazy horizon is punctuated by a prominent peak, a single soaring summit—majestic, imposing, soundless, and austere, transcending the surrounding landscape. The green foothills dramatize the sizable scale of the solitary summit, a dominating destination against which each stage of progress can be marked.

But not all mountain ranges are like the Rockies. In fact, there is another type. Take the Cascades in the Pacific Northwest, for example. The Cascades are made up of gradually rising peaks, the size and characteristics of one not revealing itself until the preceding one has been conquered, the summit being but one final stage in the gradual ascent. Aesthetically, each mountain range possesses elegance and beauty: the first is awesome and inspiring; the second, mysterious and surprising.

The two types of mountain ranges are analogous to two fundamentally different approaches to strategic change. The first is the way most companies still try to introduce large-scale, significant organizational change. The second is the way that strategic change most often actually takes place.

Traditionally, the typical organization has assumed that the business landscape, like the Rockies, is characterized by an unobscured vision of the horizon. At the outset of the strategic journey, senior management is able to scan the horizon, forecasting environmental changes that may have an impact on the company over the next several years. Assuming that these predictions will prove accurate, the firm then pinpoints a summit on the horizon, a fixed strategic objective against which organizational, managerial, and individual contributions can be assessed. It then develops a precise road map with specific routes laid out for each functional unit of the organization—marketing, research, operations, production, finance, human resources, and so on—all planned and coordinated to allow the firm to reach the strategic destination as directly and expediently as possible. Clouds of resistance, fog banks of shortsightedness, or thunderstorms of crisis might obscure the final destination now and then. But it is still assumed that the summit can and will be reached, if only the organization is persistent, maintaining its momentum and staying on course.

But successful strategic change rarely happens this way. Like a trip into the Cascades, it is usually impossible for the firm to clearly see its final destination. Clouds of swirling technological, competitive, marketplace, social, economic, and political changes often obscure an accurate view of the horizon. Until an organization takes some initial action and mounts its first hill, the size and characteristics of the next peak cannot be foreseen.

In most cases, successful strategic change comes not from compelling plans developed by heroic, charismatic leaders. Instead, fundamental organizational change most often results from journeys of learning—of setting out in a direction, of gaining new insights and making discoveries en route, of going back, adjusting old maps, developing revised plans, and taking new actions.

Evidence suggests that those companies most successful at planning and executing change did not transform themselves overnight simply by adopting the latest management innovation. Nor did they create the grand strategic plan that, through a flash of executive inspiration, produced an unparalleled competitive advantage. To paraphrase the old John Houseman television commercial, these firms made change the old-fashioned way—they learned it. Their current levels of success took many years of muddling through, of making mistakes, and of fitting the change to the organization.

For instance, after examining several companies that achieved successful breakthrough transformations, Harvard Business School professor Rosabeth Moss Kanter concludes that each success story was not the result of a "master plan" or "total program" but was, in fact, the culmination of a messy, lengthy trial-and-error process: "Xerox, Motorola, and Corning are considered exemplars of U.S. companies that have rethought their business models and renewed their organizations. Generally neglected in the accounts of successful change processes, however, is just how long it took each company to hit upon its approach and how much trial and error was involved. Corning began its partnerships five decades ago; Motorola had a participative management program in the 1970s; Xerox's companywide quality effort grew out of shaky and controversial attempts to promote employee involvement and benchmarking a dozen years ago" (1991, p. 8).

According to Kanter, although most successful strategic change occurs through a complex, trial-and-error learning process, few companies recognize that fact. Many firms actually create elaborate fictional depictions of how changes occurred. They rewrite their histories of change. They go back and simplify what actually happened to suggest that current successes resulted from great plans developed by visionary leaders and executed by skillful managers. There is good reason why. It is difficult to admit that the firm's achievements occurred through a messy learning process that no one fully comprehends and that no one can completely control. But companies can no longer afford the luxury of delusion. They must accept and embrace the fundamental truth that most change occurs through journeys of learning. It is the first step toward discovering ways to improve the capability of organizations to continuously transform themselves.

Several years ago, we conducted a study of strategic planning in approximately two hundred organizations (Redding, 1990). This study contained several surprises that altered our own opinions about organizational change. Our original intent was to determine the best ways to help companies be more successful in planning and implementing strategic change. Our approach was straightforward. We asked executives from these firms to estimate the degree to which they experienced problems planning and implementing strategic change.

As with any study, we had our hypotheses—our hunches about what we expected to find. We had two: (1) the greater the time and effort put into coming up with a plan for change, the more successful the company would be in making the plans happen; (2) the greater the attention devoted to implementing the plans, the more successful the company would be in making the plans happen. In both cases, the results were unexpected. Neither factor— the quality of the plan nor the extent of the implementation efforts—had much to do with how successful the company was in making the plans work.

What, then, accounted for the success of some change efforts and not of others? We conducted follow-up interviews with twenty firms to begin searching for other possible explanations. The following organizational characteristics were among the answers we received:

- A clear, shared idea of where the company is heading
- A spirit of experimentation and discovery
- A recognition that plans have to be continuously changed and adjusted as they go

Similar conclusions were reached in an important research study led by Michael Beer of the Harvard Business School (Beer, Eisenstat, and Spector, 1990). Beer and his associates measured the success of organizational change in six large corporations, asking why certain units were successful at change and others were not. The results were surprising, even to the researchers:

- Change efforts that begin by creating corporate programs to alter the culture or the management of people are inherently flawed even when supported by top management.
- Formal organizational structures and systems are the last things an organization should change when seeking renewal—not the first, as many managers assume.
- Effective changes in the way an organization manages people do not occur by changing the organization's human resource policies and systems.
- Starting corporate renewal at the very top is a high-risk revitalization strategy not employed by the most successful companies [Beer, Eisenstat, and Spector, 1990, p. 6].

In contrast, the most successful change efforts often started at small, peripheral parts of the organization and then gradually spread throughout the rest of the company. Plans for change were kept open and flexible. While senior management did not mandate the change, they did create a climate that demanded high performance and that encouraged the dissemination of successful innovations. This trial-and-error process, according to many, is best understood as a process of organizational learning, in which, much as do individuals, organizations learn by doing.

Parts One and Two of this book describe the process through which learning organizations mount successful strategic change. Rather than establishing formal, fixed plans through the isolated efforts of a few senior executives, learning organizations develop open, flexible plans that are fully shared and embraced by the entire organization. Rather than executing plans by the numbers, learning organizations improvise change, encouraging experimentation, rewarding small wins, and institutionalizing successes throughout the organization. Rather than reevaluating change efforts only at once-a-year planning sessions, or waiting for the slow learning that derives from experience or the traumatic learning that occurs from crisis, learning organizations build a process of reflecting and adjusting course into all change efforts. Through reflection, they seek to uncover and question the fundamental assumptions underlying original plans. They attempt to avoid simple solutions to problems, solutions that might address immediate symptoms but avoid the deeper, systemic sources of problems in the organization. And they look to expand and integrate learning by generalizing—by applying what they discover to other parts of the firm and to other problems.

Building the Readiness to Learn

By not focusing attention on the need to learn—by not building a readiness to learn—even a well-established company risks failure. The former corporate giant Pan American World Airways is a case in point.

Failing to Learn Fast Enough: The Demise of Pan American World Airways

What happened to Pan American World Airways—the innovative aviation pioneer founded in 1927 that introduced air travel across the Pacific and was the first to start commercial jet travel? Why, in 1991, was Pan Am, once "a great American institution, a symbol of American economic power" (Stern, 1991, p. 76), forced to file for bankruptcy and later sell its international routes?

Certainly deregulation was a factor. But, amid deregulation, some airlines survived, and others did not. Why was Pan Am the most notable of the casualties—not United, not American, and not Delta, the firms that vied to purchase Pan Am routes?

It was not because they didn't try. For years prior, Pan Am had engaged in ambitious efforts to enhance service quality, improve operating efficiencies, and broaden markets.

According to Newsweek, the true cause of Pan Am's demise was its failure to learn quickly enough: Pan Am "never learned how to scrap in a feistier world. Moses had to wander through the desert for 40 years. . . . [Pan Am] didn't get that much time" ("Pan American World Airways," 1991, p. 36). But, in reality, Pan Am had several decades of warning; it just never fully noticed what was going on. Early signs included rising fuel prices, mounting financial losses, stronger competition, and decreased government support years before deregulation.

In spite of these indications, Pan Am continued to act as it did before, over-purchasing 747 jets and paying too much for an ill-matched takeover of National Airlines. According to Forbes, Pan Am was doomed by its own ingrown corporate arrogance; it still perceived itself as, using its founder's words, "the chosen instrument" of the U.S. government and still acted as if its "clippers" controlled 100 percent of the Pacific market (Stern, 1991).

Initially, the idea that organizations *learn* to change sounds deceptively simple and easy. But it is not. To learn in deep and fundamental ways raises elemental fears and triggers powerful defense mechanisms. To learn means facing the unknown, recognizing that we do not possess all of the answers, conceding that we often do not know what to do, admitting that past decisions and actions may no longer be valid, questioning the basic assumptions

we have long held about running the business, and making ourselves vulnerable amid the political dynamics that pervade all
organizations. As a result, Edgar Schein (1993) observes, we often go
to extraordinary lengths to manage not to learn. We deny that problems exist. We reduce complex, multifaceted situations to simple,
either-or choices. We avoid personal responsibility by projecting
problems onto people or citing factors beyond our control.

Part Three of this book is an exploration of the specific actions many leading organizations are taking to build their readiness
to learn. Learning organizations seek to maintain and enhance a
continued state of *strategic readiness* in which entire firms—from
frontline employee to top-level executive—remain poised on the
balls of their feet, ready to act in anticipation of and in response to
unforeseen changes in their business environments and to learn
from their own experiences. By doing so, they can hopefully avoid
the need to have a looming catastrophe in order for the organization to appreciate the value of fundamental learning and change.

How do learning organizations build strategic readiness?
First, they create heightened awareness by focusing everyone's attention on the external environment, by generating a healthy dissatisfaction with the current status quo, and by developing among all
members a broad understanding of the organization as a complex,
dynamic system. Second, they make learning a way of life by developing systems that promote continuous individual learning, team
learning, and broader organization-wide learning. Finally, they become self-organizing systems that are able to continually change
shape based upon continuous learning.

Feeling Out of Control

*We once conducted a two-day workshop for managers and exec-
utives of a large manufacturing corporation experimenting with
the learning organization practices described in this book. To
begin the program, we led the group in analyzing several strategic
changes the firm had introduced over recent years, some fairly
successful, others obviously not. They included entering a new*

international market, introducing the latest generation of core products, consolidating two divisions into one, upgrading computer systems, and initiating a company-wide total quality program.

Soon, several members of the group reached the same conclusion: the varying degrees of success experienced in each of these efforts were only remotely related to the quality of the original plans or to how well these plans were implemented. Instead, their outcomes depended upon how quickly and effectively the company was able to learn from its own experiences—to begin moving in the desired direction, to encounter obstacles and surprises, to question its original strategies, to adjust course, and, throughout this process, to seize unexpected opportunities as they arose.

A manager interrupted, distraught by the implications of what he had just heard. He lamented the recent setbacks experienced by his company. The company had seemed to lose its bearings. Market share had dipped, new competitors had entered the ring, and the firm's technological edge was being dulled by "analysis paralysis." What was most needed, he felt, was for top management to lay out a clear, decisive plan of direction for the firm's future. In comparison, the notion of the learning organization seemed passive and reactive, implying that the company may be a helpless victim of its environment, incapable of making purposeful change, forced to continually react and adapt. After several minutes, his voice dropped noticeably in pitch. Offering an apologetic thank you for listening to his concerns, he said, almost in a whisper, "I'm sorry, but I feel so out of control."

Initially, the notion of the learning organization may appear to represent a slow, cumbersome, and messy way to produce organizational change. It may also seem to constitute an abdication of management responsibility by executives who equate leadership with their personal capacity to devise grand strategies, oversee their execution, and assure on-plan actions without deviation.

But, and we can not emphasize this too strongly, learning

organizations—firms that harness the power of strategic learning and build strategic readiness as a prerequisite for ongoing learning—have one purpose: to change more quickly and successfully than their competitors. And those enlightened leaders who embrace this approach to change are not abdicating their leadership responsibilities but instead are taking their duties as stewards of their organizations' futures very seriously. They just understand their roles differently, envisioning themselves not so much as great strategists and skillful administrators but as architects of strategic readiness and facilitators of strategic learning.

However, this book is not just for executives and managers. We agree with Eric Miller of the Tavistock Institute, who asserts that every member of an organization—not just senior executives—must assume responsibility for helping their organizations adapt and change as they deal with increasingly uncertain futures: "Each of us, whether on the front line or in the executive office, has two roles, each serving a different master. One in our day-to-day, narrowly defined functions. The other, as citizens of the organization, in which everyone has equal stake, equal responsibility to serve. As citizens, we question and examine the organization in terms of this open-ended, sometimes chaotic business environment, and help continue to redefine a resilient, renewing organization."[6] Therefore, we have written this book for anyone who wishes to better understand how organizations learn and who seeks to help firms to learn more quickly, deeply, and broadly than ever before.

PART ONE

FROM STRATEGIC PLANNING TO STRATEGIC LEARNING: ELEMENTS OF THE LEARNING ORGANIZATION

Change can't be transplanted. It must follow its own natural cycle of planting, growth, and harvest in each organization. In order for this to happen, the ground needs to be prepared in advance; old soil must be turned over and nourished. The seeds of change need to be sown on the organizational topsoil—the immediate issues that an organization must face. These seeds then gradually produce deep roots that wrap around the firm's management practices, business strategies, structure, and information systems. The final fruit takes its shape over the course of time. The emerging change is continuously pruned and shaped both by the natural forces of the environment and by the vigilant attention of the gardeners, who water and feed, not on a preplanned schedule but through personal judgments formed from experience and experimentation.

1

The Strategic Learning Cycle: How Organizations Learn to Change

The notion that companies plan and implement major changes in much the same way that people learn from their personal experiences may be initially hard to grasp. If so, you are probably not alone. Conceptually, it is quite a leap from learning to ride a bicycle to transforming a multi-divisional, international, diversified corporation. Or from learning to use a computer to restructuring a traditional hierarchical corporation into a flexible, responsive firm capable of continuously redefining customer expectations and quality performance.

Yet the idea that organizations learn is all around us. In fact, we frequently ask people to keep a log of the times that they hear the word *learning* as they go through each day in the firms where they work. At first, the references to learning often go unnoticed. People are so used to hearing the word that at times they miss it when it is spoken. But after a few days of persistence, it is common for people to come back with a list of dozens of references to learning in their organizations, such as the following:

"We went through quite a learning curve."
"We thought that it would be simple, but we soon learned otherwise."

>"We won't know for sure until we try it out first and learn
>   from our mistakes."
>"We have to make learning a way of life. It is the only way
>   we will survive."
>"We can learn from them, and they can learn from us."
>"What works for others won't work fot us. We'll have to
>   learn our way as we go."

Listen carefully. These are the sounds of learning in your organization.

Sometimes, these references allude to the isolated learning of
individuals. But, surprisingly, the references often pertain to the
broader, collective learning of groups or divisions in the firm, and
sometimes to the learning of the organizations at large. Intuitively,
people understand that organizations—not just individuals—learn
from their experience. This chapter will explore how the same
three-phase cycle of individual learning from our daily experiences
can be applied to the strategic learning of organizations.

The Individual Learning Cycle

Every day in every company, people learn. They acquire new
knowledge as they deal with customers and suppliers. They gather
expertise as they repeat and fine-tune their capabilities in the trial-
and-error process of making things happen. And they create new
knowledge and expertise as they confront problems and situations
never seen before.

Many leading organizations have invested a great deal in
training employees. But there is additional learning in organizations that is less visible—learning that is just as critical, if not more
so, because of its widespread pervasiveness and its job-related im-
mediacy. In fact, off-the-job training is only the very small tip of
a very large iceberg—the total learning experiences occurring within the expanse of any given organization.

If learning is an integral part of everyday experience, how
does it happen? For much of the twentieth century, attempts have
been made to better understand this elusive process. Since the time
of John Dewey, learning by doing has been represented in terms of
a cycle, moving back and forth from thought to action to reflection

and then starting over again. David Kolb (1984) represents experiential learning as a four-stage cycle of concrete experience, reflective observation, abstract conceptualization, and active experimentation. In Figure 1.1, we offer a slightly modified model of the experiential learning cycle. For example, let us consider the process by which a person might learn how to water ski.

> *Phase One: Develop a Plan.* You first develop a plan for how to water ski based on examples and suggestions—"bend your knees," "lean backwards," "keep your skis pointed straight," and so on. To do so, you may conduct a "best practices" search (looking at expert skiers) or hire a consultant (a ski instructor).
>
> *Phase Two: Implement the Plan.* After coming up with a preliminary plan for how to ski, you then go out and ski, implementing the original plan. However, despite the precision of your strategy, during your first try you find yourself falling face first into the water.
>
> *Phase Three: Reflecting on the Plan.* At that point (as you sink below the surface), you have the opportunity for learning—the occasion to reflect upon your action based

Figure 1.1. Experiential Learning Cycle.

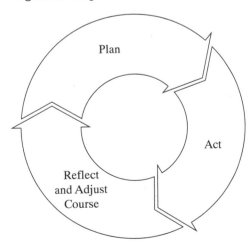

upon what worked and what did not, to question your
original assumptions, and to alter your initial plan in
response.

Over the next several iterations of this learning cycle (and
several more premature dunks), your plan becomes increasingly refined—"lean back exactly this far," "bend your knees like this,"
"keep the tips of the skis pointed up," and so on. The learning
continues, and, cycle after cycle, your skiing improves. In the beginning, you just wanted to get up on the skis. Then you aspired to
stay up, remaining secure in the predictable, smooth path cut by the
towing boat. But over time, you are able to begin to explore, turning
out across the wake, challenging the bumps, and accelerating your
speed.

Today, organizations are increasingly recognizing the importance of the ongoing, day-to-day learning. In fact, Reg Revans
suggests that learning by doing is a primordial force of nature and
the driving energy behind natural evolution: "We may all agree that
learning by doing is, in many forms, nothing very new. It is one of
the primary forces of evolution, and has accompanied mankind
since long before our ancestors came down from the trees. Even the
most primitive creatures must have learnt from their own experience, by carrying on what they found good for them and by re-
fraining from what they found to be harmful" (1991, p. 3).

While not new, learning from experience is increasingly essential as rapid rates of change cause people to be confronted with
situations nobody has faced before. In many cases, answers from the
past cannot be used to provide solutions for the future. Training
and education are useful methods to discover what is known. However, they are becoming less and less relevant as people are faced
with unknown features that compel them to invent new knowledge
and skills.

The Strategic Learning Cycle

Just as everyday people learn from their experiences, so do organizations. In fact, as we noted earlier, it is possible to understand

strategic planning as a process of organizational learning (de Geus, 1988).

Strategic planning has been around for about a generation, offering a powerful means for anticipating and adapting to dynamic business conditions. In most cases, strategic planning occurs on an annual rolling cycle, often with a horizon of three to five years. Each year, participants start by studying the business environment, gathering information on environmental trends that are impacting or may impact the organization. Then, choosing from a variety of planning tools and techniques (such as portfolio grids and life cycles), the firm selects the best possible strategy that, building upon the organization's strengths and competencies, affords a defensible competitive position given the forecasted changes. These are then transformed into objectives, strategies, and plans that are documented in a formal written business plan. Each year, the plan is reexamined and modified based upon new information.

Strategic planning was and continues to be the most popular form of business planning. There are good reasons why. Strategic planning is rational, stressing objective data gathering, systematic analysis, and detailed planning. Strategic planning provides senior management with the ability to understand and decode complex business conditions. Moreover, strategic planning offers the promise of quick, concrete results.

But today, strategic planning is under attack. According to *Fortune* magazine, "Strategic planning has become overly bureaucratic, absurdly quantitative, and largely irrelevant. In executive suites across America, countless five year plans, updated annually and solemnly clad in three-ring binders, are gathering dust, their impossibly specific prognostications about costs, prices, and market share long forgotten" (Henkoff, 1990, p. 70). Even *Planning Review*, the journal of the International Society for Strategic Management and Planning, wonders if "strategizing as we know it become[s] obsolete in today's chaotic environment" (Reimann and Ramanujam, 1992, p. 36).

There is considerable evidence to support these criticisms of strategic planning. Even with the most sensitive and sophisticated environmental scanning methods, organizations are often confronted with unforeseen events. Even when firms possess advance intelligence or insight regarding future changes, they often fail to act on the new information since it challenges prevailing organizational mind-sets. Moreover, by the time plans are formulated and implemented, they are no longer relevant. Competition has acted too quickly. Customer expectations have shifted too dramatically. And the marketplace has experienced unexpected turns. Before the firm has perceived what is happening—and more importantly, acted on it—the future has passed by.

From our perspective, sounding the death knell for strategic planning is premature. Organizations need to continue to identify environmental trends and strategize for the future. The problem is not with strategic planning itself. It is with the arrogant assumption that executives can gaze into a crystal ball and forecast the future. It is with the limited, restricted, and linear approach to strategic planning that is in search of creating "the great master plan." It is with the simplistic notion that once senior management has endorsed a plan, implementation will be easy.

Strategic change rarely happens that way. In most cases, according to Henry Mintzberg and James Waters, a business strategy is less the direct result of deliberate plans than it is a process of strategic learning:

> The fundamental difference between deliberate and emergent strategy is that whereas the former focuses on direction and control—getting desired things done—the latter opens up the notion of "strategic learning." Defining strategy as intended and conceiving it as deliberate, as has traditionally been done, effectively precludes the notion of strategic learning. Once the intentions have been set, attention is riveted on realizing them, not on adapting them. Messages from the environment tend to get blocked out. . . . Emergent strategy itself implies learning what works—taking one action at a time in search for that viable pattern or consistency. It is important to remember that emergent strategy means, not chaos, but in essence, *unintended order*. . . . This is another way of saying that not a few deliberate strategies are simply

emergent ones that have been uncovered and subsequently formalized [1985, pp. 270–271].

Take a look at the strategic changes that your organization has sought to make over recent years. It is likely that the success of one change effort over another has little to do with the quality of the original plans. Or even how well these plans were initially implemented. Instead, it is most likely that their outcomes depended upon how quickly and effectively the firm was able to begin moving in the desired direction, to encounter obstacles and surprises, to question its original strategies, to adjust course, and, throughout this process, to seize unexpected opportunities as they arose.

How does this strategic learning process take place? In our view, through the same three-phase cycle—planning, implementing, reflecting—that we used to explain how people learn how to water ski. Richard Normann explains:

> Strategic action is rarely a simple sequence of "first decision, then action." This "sequence myth" has done a lot of damage to many business companies. . . . Instead, we can observe how strategies evolve as a result of a process that has at least three key elements: the formulation of a vision, action based on that vision, and interpretation and reflection based on the action and its outcome. Then the sequence starts again: The vision is further clarified, new action is taken, there is food for more reflection, and so on. There are few instances of strategic change that are not best described in terms of such a spiraling process [1985, p. 220].

This three-phase strategic learning cycle is shown in Figure 1.2.

Continuous Planning

Traditionally, organizations have relied upon formal, written, detailed programs and procedures to communicate what needs to be

Figure 1.2. Strategic Learning Cycle.

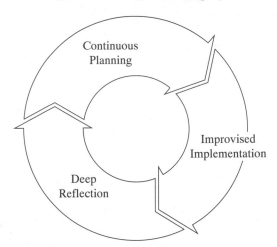

changed. In contrast, in learning organizations, fixed plans are displaced by flexible, open strategic directions. They are not merely envisioned and planned by top management but are fully embraced and shared by people involved in making them happen.

Strategic plans are essential for strategic change. Organizations must analyze the information about their environments, chart strategic directions, and develop goals and plans for future change. In learning organizations, however, planning is a continuous, evolving process, with plans being questioned, refined, and modified based upon the most current information about environments as well as through insights gained from implementation efforts. As a result, in learning organizations, *re-vision* may be more important than *vision*. Planning is seen as an open process, involving the participation of people throughout the organizations as well as key stakeholders (suppliers, customers, and so on) from outside the firms.

Improvised Implementation

Once plans are developed, they need to be executed. In learning organizations, the act of implementation differs greatly from the way it works in traditional organizations, which rely on formal, written, detailed procedures to communicate and spell out how plans are to be implemented. Instead, in learning organizations, individuals and teams act in creative, autonomous, and spontaneous ways to interpret the strategic direction and make the plans happen.

Most successful change efforts start through the proliferation of a large number of modest experiments and grass-roots innovations, the most successful of which are promoted throughout the company (Kanter, 1991). Doing so reduces the risks and resistance inherent in broad-scale strategic change. The actual nature of a strategic change is gradually revealed through the actions of people throughout the firm who are trying to make change happen. Through this process, people discover for themselves over time that change is in their best interests and that the benefits outweigh the risks, such as the potential loss of power, status, security, and expected career progressions. Over time, successes and accomplishments are reinforced and institutionalized, modifying the formal structures, rewards, procedures, and systems of organizations.

Deep Reflection

In learning organizations, learning is not something that just happens. It is made to happen. Learning begins when those involved in an activity stop and examine how things are being done. In learning organizations, attempts are made to provide frequent, ongoing opportunities for reflective learning. Learning organizations do not wait for problems or crises to compel reevaluation. Reflection becomes part of "the way we do things around here" and is built into the implementation of strategic change. Through this process, learning organizations endeavor to question basic beliefs and search for systemic solutions to present problems.

Traditional strategic planning provides firms with limited opportunities for reflection. There is often but one planned iteration of the learning cycle per year. Otherwise, organizations stop and examine implementation activities only when obvious roadblocks appear. As a result, competitive positioning, technological mastery, and strategic responses can often take many years, and sometimes decades, to achieve or to yield results.

Learning organizations, on the other hand, continuously take action, reflect upon that action, and modify plans based on insights gained through this learning process. The aim is to maximize the speed and effectiveness of strategic change by incorporating reflection into all change efforts and not waiting for the next annual planning cycle or for a crisis to demand reevaluation. Each iteration of the learning process starts with the act of reflection, stepping back, if just for a moment, and asking, "To what degree are we accomplishing not just what we set out to do but what we need to accomplish given what we know today?" The next step is to examine roadblocks by questioning original assumptions and developing deep, systemic solutions to newly emerging problems. Insights gained through this process are then used to modify the original plans. In addition, whenever possible, these learnings are generalized to other changes being attempted in the organization, even those that possess little surface similarity to the original change.

In this chapter, we depicted the process of strategic change as a three-phase learning cycle. Similarly, Charles Handy (1990) pictures learning, whether by individuals or organizations, as a wheel: "I describe it as a wheel to emphasize that it is meant to go round and round. . . . It is life's special treadmill. Step off of it and you ossify. . . . The trouble is that for most of us for much of the time the wheel does not go round. It gets stuck or blocked" (pp. 58–59). Learning organizations engage in sustained and continuous activities to keep the wheel of learning turning quickly and smoothly. How that is done is the subject of the next chapter.

2

Speed, Depth, and Breadth: How Organizations Accelerate Learning

Central to our conception of learning organizations is the notion of *iteration*. An iteration refers to each 360 degree rotation through the planning-implementing-reflecting learning cycle. It is interesting to note that the term iteration derives from the Latin word *iter*, which means journey, way, or road. Therefore, iteration, as we use it, refers not to a continuous repetition of an unaltered pattern. Rather, it denotes the process through which organizations move in a desired strategic direction through cycles of learning. In this way, iterations of learning cycles—and not detailed action plans and programs for change—represent the paths to the future in learning organizations. In learning organizations, change is cyclical and not linear. Therefore, change must be measured through circles and not straight lines.

Looking closely at each iteration of the learning cycle, it is possible to delineate three separate factors that determine the effectiveness of strategic learning:

- The *speed* of learning—how fast organizations are able to rotate around the learning cycle. In other words, speed refers to the number of iterations through the learning cycle in a given period of time.
- The *depth* of learning—the degree to which organizations are

able to learn at the end of each iteration of the cycle by questioning underlying assumptions.
- The *breadth* of learning—how extensively organizations are able to transfer the new insights and knowledge derived from each iteration of the learning cycle to other issues and parts of their firms.

Speed, depth, and breadth constitute the three dimensions of strategic learning. Learning organizations continuously seek to improve all three. To explain what we mean, an illustration may be useful. In fact, in this chapter, we provide two. The first represents a learning cycle as it might typically occur in an organization. The second demonstrates how a similar cycle might unfold in an organization that is intentionally seeking to improve and accelerate its learning.

A Tale of Two Cycles: Example One

In the case of one company, the learning process was not dissimilar to that undertaken by most traditional organizations.

Planning

During an annual strategic planning session, senior management decided that the company could meet long-term competitive challenges only by significantly upgrading its technical and professional capabilities in two areas: research and development and international marketing. To do so, the firm would need an ambitious recruiting and hiring program, attracting the highest-quality, most experienced professionals in both of these areas. These people would also need to be able to work effectively with the "old-timers," who were known as the best operational and administrative people in the industry.

Yet there was a potential problem. Over the past few years, the company had hired several first-rate professionals, people exactly like those now needed, but the firm was not able to keep them. In fact, several of the people did not seem to fit in well and struggled with getting up to speed and learning how things were done in the company. Very few made it beyond the first year.

In response, as part of the company's strategic plan, an objective was set to improve hiring and reduce turnover. To achieve these two goals, improving the interviewing skills of managers was deemed to be essential. In addition, an effective, structured orientation process was felt to be necessary to help the new hires get off on the right foot. Both of these tactics were included as part of the strategic plan.

Implementation

The human resource group was charged with making these plans happen. Over the next six months, and with the help of key line managers, they developed detailed profiles of the specific skills and knowledge the new staff would need, and they designed an intensive interviewing skills program for managers to improve their abilities to select the best candidates. Eighty percent of managers participated in the training, and the program seemed to be well received.

At the same time, a new orientation program was implemented. Each new person was provided an intensive overview of company operations, rotating around from department to department to understand how things worked. The new hire was also paired with a mentor, an experienced, proven person of similar professional or technical background who would help the new person get going.

Reflection

At the company's next annual planning meeting, senior management asked for turnover data from the past year. To their surprise, the turnover rate for the new hires was still extremely high despite the interviewing skills training and the orientation program. Moreover, several managers said that the new people were just not working out.

The human resource group investigated the reason why

turnover was still so high. Two people were assigned to evaluate the interviewing skills program and two others to examine the orientation program. A week later, the two groups reported. Most managers were not using the skills taught in the interviewing program and had reverted back to old habits. Moreover, only slightly more than half of the new employees completed the orientation program as designed, apparently because managers did not want to release the new people from their jobs to attend orientation meetings, and because the mentors were too valuable to be allowed time away from their own projects and responsibilities.

Presenting these findings to the executive team, the human resource group recommended that senior managers conduct at least one employment interview with each subordinate manager to ensure that effective interviewing practices were being carried out. In addition, they suggested that the orientation process be modified to be more workable. Three people would be designated as mentors each year and would be assigned a reduced project load as a result. In addition, they asked that executives talk to each of the supervisors of the new employees to let them know how important it was to fully complete the orientation program as designed. Everyone agreed to these recommendations.

Three Dimensions of Strategic Learning

Before discussing this case illustration, let us briefly examine each of the three dimensions of learning—speed, depth, and breadth.

Speed of Learning

The first dimension of strategic learning is the speed of the iterations of the learning cycle (see Figure 2.1).

Learning organizations seek to increase the speed at which learning happens by reducing the cycle time of learning iterations. Each iteration is an opportunity for learning. Each time that the organization develops a plan, implements the plan, and then stops and reflects on what has worked and what has not worked, there is

Figure 2.1. Speed of Strategic Learning.

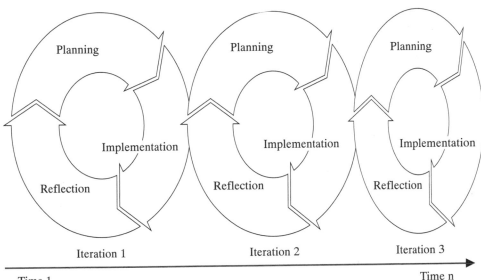

Planning

Implementation

Reflection

Iteration 1

Planning

Implementation

Reflection

Iteration 2

Planning

Implementation

Reflection

Iteration 3

Time 1

Time n

Speed

an opportunity for learning. Simply stated, if a firm can get around the circle faster, it will have increased its chances to learn.

Yet, traditionally, the cycle times of strategic learning have been fairly lengthy in most organizations. In most cases, iterations of the learning cycle are limited to once-a-year reviews and revisions of strategic plans during annual strategic planning sessions. At the start of the year, strategic plans are developed, often with three- to five-year planning horizons. Throughout the course of the year, these plans are implemented. A year later, the plans are reexamined and updated, with the planning horizon extended out one more year. During the year, there may be periodic reviews of the plans, but these reviews often do not represent true iterations of the strategic learning cycle. That is, they often do not include serious reflection upon the validity of the plans themselves. Any serious questioning of original assumptions is avoided. Instead, these reviews are usually limited to working out the details of implementation and enforcing compliance with the plan as originally developed. The only time that plans are seriously reviewed and questioned during the year is when major problems or crises arise. At these points, companies are forced to stop, to admit that something is not working, and to reexamine their strategies and plans.

In contrast, learning organizations seek to accelerate the cycle times of strategic learning. To do so, they are action oriented in all three phases: planning, implementation, and reflection. Not waiting for annual planning retreats to compel reevaluation, they make planning-implementation-reflection an ongoing process throughout the year. Plans are always open and subject to review. Implementation is focused on quick action to provide the information needed to clarify strategic direction. And reflection is built into all strategic change from the beginning and recognized as being of equal importance to planning and implementation in ensuring success.

Depth of Learning

The second dimension of strategic learning is the depth of questioning that occurs as the firm reflects upon its actions and modifies its original plans. The depth of questioning determines the level of learning that occurs during each iteration (see Figure 2.2). The depth of learning tends to increase along with the number of iterations of the learning cycle.

Fast cycle time does not guarantee learning. It merely provides the opportunity for learning. Just because the three-phase cycle of planning-implementing-reflecting is complete, it does not necessarily guarantee that learning occurs. Nor does it indicate how deeply organizations are able to learn.

Taking the lead of Argyris and Schön (1978), we distinguish three levels of organizational learning:

> *Level One: Symptomatic Learning.* Learning that provides simple solutions to the problems and roadblocks encountered, resolving obvious symptoms. Argyris and Schön (1978) call this *single-loop learning.*
> *Level Two: Systemic Learning.* Learning that provides deeper, systemic solutions to the problems and roadblocks en-

Figure 2.2. Depth of Strategic Learning.

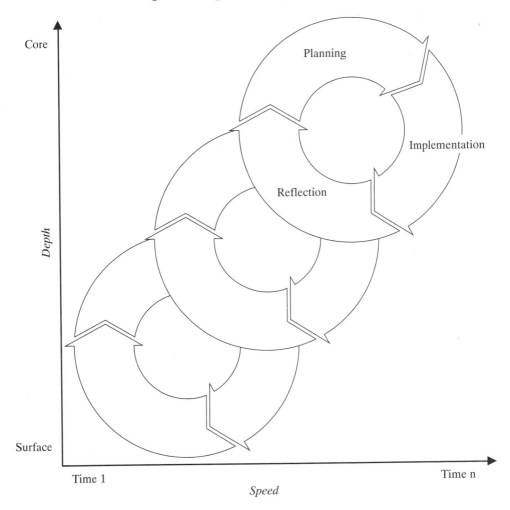

countered, often resulting in the need to modify the fundamental norms, management practices, procedures, structures, and processes of the organization. This is Argyris and
Schön's *double-loop learning.*

Level Three: Learning to Learn. Learning that serves to evaluate and improve the learning process itself. Argyris and
Schön label it *deutero-learning.*

The major difference among the three levels of learning is the quality of questioning that occurs during the reflection phase. At the first level, questioning is limited to fine-tuning the original plans in response to the impediments being encountered in making plans happen. As a result, first-level learning deals with fixing the immediate problems at hand; it may not confront the root-cause issues that may be contributing to problems. At the second level, deeper questions are raised regarding how current difficulties may be symptomatic of pervasive, systemic issues, such as organizational norms, management styles, information systems, processes, and procedures. As a result, organizations have the opportunity to learn about themselves as complex systems, and fairly routine problems, when understood as symptoms of deeper causal factors, can provide the basis for truly effective strategic learning. At the third level, questions are raised about the learning process itself, exploring the effectiveness with which organizations are able to learn. This third "learning to learn" level provides the possibility for the deepest form of organizational learning, increasing the core capacity of firms to learn regardless of the strategic issue at hand.

To increase the depth of learning, organizations must encourage and value questioning. As managers, we sometimes think that it is our responsibility to have the answers—to know what to do, how to do it, and how to measure that it has been done. Instead, we need to develop our tolerance for ambiguity; we need to give ourselves the freedom to not have all the answers and to learn from our mistakes. Charles Handy, borrowing from the poet John Keats, encourages us all to develop what he calls negative capability:

> Keats defined *negative capability* . . . as "when a man is capable of being in uncertainties, mysteries, and doubts." I would extend the meaning to include the capacity to live with mistakes and failures without being downhearted or dismayed.
>
> Learning and changing are never clear and never sure. Whenever we change, we step out a little into the unknown. We will never know enough about that unknown to be certain of the result. We will get it wrong some of the time. Doubts and mistakes must not be

allowed to disturb us because it is from them that we
learn. Theories are no good . . . unless it is possible to
prove them wrong. If they are bound to be right, they
are either tautologies, saying nothing useful, or trivial,
saying nothing important [1990, pp. 68–69].

By cultivating negative capability, we can look at our mistakes as
opportunities for learning.

Moreover, learning organizations attempt to build an environment in which it is safe, both psychologically and politically, to
question the rules of the game, even when the rules seem to work.
By taking the spirit of continuous improvement embraced in recent
quality improvement efforts and transferring that spirit to the
broadest, most crucial issues facing the organization, learning organizations acknowledge that "we can always get better." In stable,
simple environments, companies can develop game plans, stick to
them, and feel fairly secure. But since, for most firms today, playing
fields are constantly shifting, learning organizations continually
seek to ask the toughest questions about the rules of the game. It
is the freedom to question firms' most basic assumptions that promotes the deepest, most effective strategic learning.

Breadth of Learning

The third dimension of strategic learning is the breadth of learning
(Figure 2.3). At the conclusion of each iteration of the strategic
learning cycle, certain insights are derived that may have application to other issues and to other parts of the organization. The
breadth of learning is the degree to which learning is successfully
integrated throughout the organization. As shown in Figure 2.3, the
breadth of learning tends to increase, as does the depth of learning,
as the number of learning cycles increases.

The transfer and dissemination of knowledge across a highly
differentiated and often conflict-ridden organization challenges
firms to learn by extrapolation and collaboration. For instance, if
a firm gains insight into a specific international market, is that
knowledge transferred to other divisions also seeking to enter or
expand that market? Or if one part of the company is struggling to

Figure 2.3. Breadth of Strategic Learning.

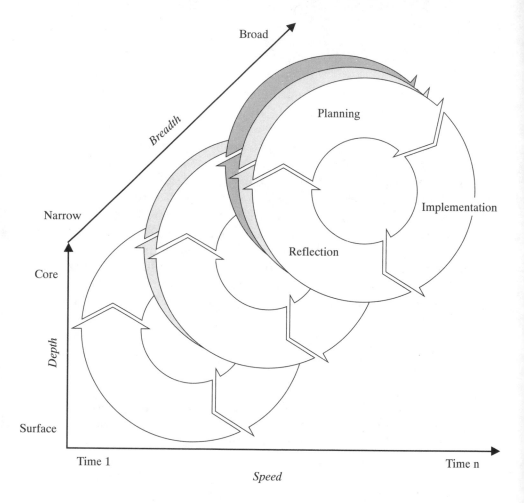

conquer some particularly stubborn technological roadblock, does it look to the collective knowledge of the entire firm, including its suppliers and customers, to see what has been learned from previous experience? Learning organizations are effective at taking knowledge gained in one area and utilizing it in other parts of the organization facing similar challenges.

But there is another aspect to broadening strategic learning:

taking the insights derived from experience with a specific problem and applying those discoveries to dissimilar issues. Why would the learning derived from one problem apply to another? Because organizations are complex, interrelated systems. The same underlying issue (such as a short-term mind-set or an aversion to risk taking) that is affecting the company's ability to introduce a new product or adopt a new technology may be equally relevant to improving customer service or forming a new strategic alliance. If people can stop and ask, "You know, is there anything we discovered from X that might apply to Y?" they might minimize the need to make the same mistake again.

Learning can be broadened by promoting open and collaborative exchanges of ideas between individuals, teams, and divisions, and even with suppliers, customers, and competitors. The importance of taking the lessons learned in one area and applying them to another area or another issue becomes evident when we view organizations as open systems. The testing of ideas in new settings often expands our understanding by helping to clarify what we know and what we think we know. Applying our knowledge to a broader, more diverse range of problems helps organizations to learn by leveraging old knowledge into new understandings.

We have separately discussed each of the three dimensions of learning—speed, depth, and breadth. But the three are not entirely discrete. They are related to each other. Increased speed fosters increased depth. Increased depth leads to increased breadth. Let us explain. If there are more iterations of the learning cycle, it is more likely that the firm will realize the limitations of Level One solutions that only address the symptoms and not the underlying causes. As problems continue to persist from one iteration to the next, there is an enhanced likelihood that the firm will appreciate deeper learnings—Levels Two and Three—that get below the surface, seeking out the underlying reasons for the difficulties. Moreover, as more profound learnings occur, the solutions will deal with the more systemic issues of the organization. And since systemic issues often have impact upon a wide range of organizational issues in varying parts of the firm, there is an increased likelihood that the new knowledge will more easily transfer to other issues or parts of the company.

So now let us return to the illustration entitled "A Tale of Two Cycles: Example One" that started this chapter. How effective was the learning in this cycle?

Speed. The speed of learning was slow. It took a full year to complete the first iteration of the learning cycle.

Depth. The depth of learning was limited. It dealt only with addressing the symptoms at hand, not raising any fundamental questions about the original assumption that interviewing skills and poor orientation were the causes of high turnover.

Breadth. The breadth of learning was narrow. There was no attempt to take the new insights from this learning cycle and apply it to other issues or other parts of the organization. For example, were there other training programs that were well received but that were not being applied back on the job?

A Tale of Two Cycles: Example Two

Now, let us look at this same situation in an organization that has developed its strategic learning capability in all three areas: speed, depth, and breadth.

Planning

The basic scenario is the same as that in the first example. At the annual strategic planning meeting, an objective was set to increase the firm's research and development and international marketing expertise. To minimize turnover, it would provide interviewing skills training and a more structured approach to the new employee's orientation program.

At this meeting, however, several senior managers asked for more information about the reasons the company had been losing so many new professional staff. Not everyone was con-

vinced that improved interviewing skills and a more formal orientation program would help. But they agreed to give these solutions a try. It was determined that both programs would be piloted over the next three months. The executive team agreed to meet again in exactly three months to review the results from the pilot projects.

Implementation

A pilot interviewing program and a pilot orientation program were implemented within a month. A month later the human resource group established a committee of managers, new hires, and "old-timers" to assess the progress and to see what was working and what was not.

Reflection

At the first meeting of the committee, the human resource group provided information that showed that new employees were still experiencing discomfort with learning the new jobs and that managers were still feeling that it was taking too long for the people to get up to speed.

In discussing the information, it became clear that several managers did not agree with the original assumptions: (1) that they were selecting the wrong people because of a lack of interviewing skills, and (2) that new people were not receiving adequate orientation and training during the first few months. After about a half hour, one manager who had been quiet said, "I probably shouldn't say this, but I don't think we are paying new people enough." The reaction of the group was immediate. Several people strongly disagreed, and soon the topic was changed back to a discussion of merits of the training and orientation programs.

A few minutes later, the leader of the meeting said, "I think we passed over Bill's comment about pay pretty quickly. Bill, could you talk about that a little more?"

"Isn't it true," Bill started, with an obvious hesitation in his

voice, "that there is an unwritten rule in the company that you can't pay new people more than the current people performing similar jobs? This stops us from getting the best people and paying them what they can get paid someplace else."

"Yes," a voice shot back, "and that's the way it should be. Why should new people get paid more than those of us who've been here for years?"

"Just bear with me," Bill continued. "Yet our aim is to hire people with more experience and better technical backgrounds. It sounds like a dilemma. We want increased expertise, yet we can't pay for it. So one of two things happens. We hire people who aren't exactly what we are looking for and who therefore have trouble meeting our expectations. We make them feel like failures, and they soon leave us. Or even when they are successful, they always have the possibility of getting paid more elsewhere. And with their professional and technical backgrounds, they usually have no problem finding another job. No wonder new people are dissatisfied and turnover is high."

Bill had uncovered a strong, unstated norm of internal equity in the organization and revealed it: new people should never be compensated more than current employees, even when they bring enhanced talent to the organization.

Over the next several meetings of the committee, there were heated debates about the issue of paying new hires more than their colleagues. After a few meetings, the group discovered a creative solution when it was recognized that there are ways to reward people other than just through their salaries. They agreed to keep the base pay the same for new hires and current staff while offering increased incentives and bonuses for specific contributions to achieving the company's research and development and international marketing objectives. The committee also discussed nonmonetary ways of rewarding the new employees. Since the new hires valued professional development strongly, increased efforts would be made to provide opportunities for continuing professional growth and recognition.

These recommendations were presented to the executive staff at the three-month follow-up meeting. By the time of the *next annual strategic planning meeting, the new compensation system for new technical and professional staff had been piloted and its results evaluated. With some modifications, the program was approved for a rollout to all current employees, as well as all new hires.*

In addition, the committee provided a proposal for an expanded recognition program for veteran employees. In their discussions, the committee revealed that many old employees felt they were no longer being valued by the company. All the attention was going to the "techies," as the new professional staff were called. That is why there was so much concern about equal pay. The committee concluded that recognizing the contributions of all employees would reduce the inevitable tension between the new hires and the veterans. The members had discovered that the maxim "money isn't everything" was true not only for the new employees but for everyone.

In comparing the two learning cycle examples, it is obvious that the second example is characterized by increased speed, depth, and breadth of learning.

Speed. In the first example, it took a year for a full iteration of the strategic learning cycle to take place; in the second, just a few months.

Depth. In the first example, solutions were limited to addressing the symptoms. In the second, the original underlying assumptions were challenged, leading to more powerful solutions.

Breadth. In the first example, there was little transfer of learning. In the second, the discovery of the importance of nonfinancial rewards ("money isn't everything") was applied to everyone in the company, not just the new hires.

Learning organizations seek to continuously enhance the speed, depth, and breadth of strategic learning. To promote speed, learning organizations are action oriented when it comes to strategic change. To promote depth, learning organizations question fundamental assumptions. And to promote breadth, learning organizations seek to integrate the learning that happens in one part of the organizations with one issue and transfer those insights to other divisions and other problems.

3

Strategic Readiness: How Organizations Prepare to Learn

What does it take for organizations to learn in deep and fundamental ways? We believe that firms require a heightened state of *strategic readiness*.

To a large degree, individuals cannot learn until they are ready to learn. The same is true for organizations. Pfeiffer and Jones (1978) stated, "Once an individual child is ready to read, it is somewhat immaterial which teaching method is used. Conversely when a child is not ready to learn to read, all strategies are relatively unsuccessful in teaching that child how to read. In an analogous way, once an organizational system has the necessary prerequisites, change is likely to take place regardless of which methodology is applied. Conversely, the most sophisticated techniques employed by the most competent and experienced consultants and managers are doomed to failure when the organization itself is unready to undertake a project of planned change" (p. 219).

The degree to which readiness is present at any given moment in a firm's history will significantly determine how well it learns from its own experience and adapts in anticipation of and in response to environmental challenges. And the relative degrees of readiness of two organizations determines, to a large extent, the differences in their abilities to learn quickly from internal and external changes.

Strategic Readiness at TRW Space and Defense

*With the collapse of the USSR and Eastern Europe, and with ac-
companying fluctuations in government spending, the defense
industry was up for grabs. No one knew what would happen next.
Would a period of relative peace sweep across the world, with the
United States needing only a fraction of its current military
strength to maintain needed superiority? Would Yeltsin be over-
thrown in Russia and a new government take over, providing a
heightened military threat to the United States and its allies?
Would regional conflicts, such as those in the Persian Gulf and
Yugoslavia, demand a strong U.S. defense presence and create an
increased international demand for arms?*

*A few years ago, as the full scope of this global sea change
was first being fathomed, we had the opportunity to interview
members of several defense industry companies, including
General Dynamics, McDonnell-Douglas, Lockheed, and TRW.
Each of these firms was facing relatively similar uncertainties, yet
the responses were not at all the same.*

*Despite the evidence—and this might be surprising—some
organizations were still fairly complacent, carrying on business as
usual. In one firm, for instance, there was widespread resistance
to biting the bullet and making adjustments close to home, even
though most managers understood the potential impact of the
environmental changes, at least in an abstract sense. Moreover,
the full understanding of the need to change was limited to management, with little or no formal communication of the realities
of business conditions to the work force at large. And with many
employees with twenty-five or more years of seniority, there was
a widespread feeling that "things won't change until the old guys
retire."*

*Other firms were in shock. Staff layoffs had become com-
monplace. Plans targeted several plants to be shut down, but nobody knew which ones, since political considerations (such as the
power of congressmen to keep plants in their districts) were driving the decisions. Strategic planning was restricted to a small*

group of senior executives. Within this context, rumors were spreading like wildfire, including one that the company was being sold to a chief competitor.

But there was also a third group of companies—firms embarked upon ambitious efforts to prepare themselves for the "brave new world" of the future, even when they were unsure what exactly would happen. An example is the TRW Space and Defense Group, the world's largest producer of surveillance satellites. Starting as early as the mid 1980s, the TRW Space and Defense Group had been engaged in continuous, ambitious efforts to prepare itself to be successful, no matter what happened. To do so, it took several major actions.

One of these initiatives was to create a collective, organization-wide awareness of the need for fundamental change. TRW took steps to communicate to everyone the factors that were combining to make the future so troublesome, including:

- A potentially significant decline in defense spending
- A complete dislocation of high-tech personnel in terms of job requirements, pay, and benefits
- A smarter customer set who would want much more for much less

People throughout the firm then began constructing potential scenarios of the future. According to one manager, "That was where much of the learning took place. Everyone got involved, and this added to the alignment and buy-in later on. So when we came out and started talking about specific changes, even threatening changes, people went 'Ah,' and their buy-in time was much shorter because they saw where the change came from."

TRW also developed the flexibility to act and react quickly. It set out to increase the adaptability of the company's core processes and technologies, as well as the capabilities of its work force. An early focus of effort was called the common satellite bus system. Previously, TRW had produced each satellite from scratch. By creating a common chassis (bus), TRW could reduce manufacturing cycle time and quickly adapt its technology to a wide va-

riety of different uses. For example, if defense expenditures for satellites were to be drastically cut, TRW could be able to quickly shift its production capacity to applications outside the defense industry. In addition to developing the common satellite bus system, TRW broadened the capabilities of its work force so skills could be applied to a wide range of needs. Today, TRW has in place an ongoing process of redesign, aimed at continuously enhancing the flexibility of the organization.

Another TRW action was to build its capacity to obtain knowledge, integrate it, and disseminate it across the organization. To do so, the company implemented an electronic "neural network" using electronic mail. Anyone could connect into it. At first, there was an information explosion. But now the amount of data is manageable, and daily communication through E-mail as a means of organizational learning has become a way of life. In addition to computerized neural networks, TRW established similar networks through face-to-face, informal communication. For instance, regular meetings were set up to include both procurement and engineering personnel. They focused on identifying what each group had learned recently, which new technologies were on the horizon, and what competitors were up to. The two groups also established a future learning agenda—issues that were most important to learn about in the future.

So far, the results of TRW's readiness initiatives are impressive. There have been no major layoffs. And the time to get products to market has been slashed from forty-five to twenty-one months. But TRW feels it still has not reached the point at which it wants to be—where one member's getting pricked makes the whole organization say, "Ouch!"[1]

All companies learn from their experiences. The problem is that they rarely learn fast enough, because old mind-sets about the business, about "how we do things around here," about "what makes us successful," often get in the way. The often-told boiled-frog story provides an apt analogy, illustrating the power of these collective mind-sets. Place a frog in a pan of room temperature water, and it will sit there. Put the pan on a stove, and gradually raise the temperature of the water. The frog will still stay put, slowly adapting to the rising temperature. In fact, even as the temperature rises high enough to boil it to death, the frog will remain in the water, content, continuously adapting to the gradual increases in temperature. As long as the adjustments happen slowly enough, the frog will fail to react.

Many companies today are boiling frogs. They are not complacent, nor are they stagnant. They are highly skilled at slow and incremental learning and adaptation. However, by the time that the changes in their environments have an impact, it is too late to jump out of the pot. The water is already boiling. They failed to recognize the potential effects of the shifts in their environments and to modify their fundamental understandings of the situation.

The learning organization engages in extensive activities to prepare the organization as a whole to learn. In learning organizations, building strategic readiness is not a one-time event designed to prepare the organization for a specific change. Instead, readiness consists of a perpetual state of preparedness for change in general; amid highly turbulent conditions, the organization needs to be equipped to deal with anything and must be ready to reevaluate old assumptions and adjust its plans for the future.

Unfreezing Organizations

In seeking an answer to the question of why some organizations change successfully while others don't, we might begin by considering Kurt Lewin's model (1951) of organizational change. According to Lewin, for companies to change, they must undergo a three-phase process of *unfreezing-changing-refreezing* as follows:

1. Organizations function for prolonged periods of time in relatively *frozen* states in which fundamental norms, structures, processes, and systems are left unquestioned and consequently, unaltered. During these periods, organizational changes are *within the frame,* restricted to incremental improvements targeted at doing what the company already does, but doing it more efficiently and effectively.

    2.   Fundamental, frame-breaking change occurs only during relatively brief transitional periods when firms, challenged by circumstances that demand that they modify their basic ways of doing business, become *unfrozen* and raise elemental questions about the soundness of organizational purposes, processes, procedures, structures, and systems.

    3.   Once these brief episodes of change have terminated and new, more successful organizational patterns have been discovered, firms then *refreeze* again into new, more successful states, incorporating these changes into a new equilibrium.

From Lewin's perspective, the history of most firms is characterized by extended eras of equilibrium, punctuated by brief transitional states of transformation.

    What does it mean to say a company is frozen? Frozen states are characterized by a community—a collective entity—embracing a central set of assumptions and beliefs that, in everyday language, represent "the way we do things around here" and "what has made us successful." These shared understandings suggest provisional answers to a broad range of questions, such as, What products should we manufacture, and how should we produce them? Who are our customers, and what do they expect? Who are our competitors, and how should we deal with them? What suppliers should we use, and what should we require of them? What technologies should be employed? How should we be structured? How should we communicate? How should we make decisions? and so on.

    The shared assumptions serve a purpose. During periods of relative environmental calm, they protect the firm from disruptive, unnecessary, counterproductive self-examination, and they allow the organization to concentrate upon maximizing its strengths. Thomas Kuhn (1970), in analyzing major scientific discoveries, such as the breakthroughs of Copernicus, Galileo, and Einstein, called such a prevailing set of assumptions and beliefs a paradigm: "The term *paradigm* is used in two different senses. On the one hand, it stands for the entire constellation of beliefs, values, techniques, and so on shared by the members of a given community. On the other hand, it denotes one sort of element in that constellation, the concrete puzzle-solutions which, employed as models or examples, can replace explicit rules as a basis for the solution of the remaining puzzles" (p. 175).

While Kuhn used the term *paradigm,* others prefer *mind-sets* (Pascale, 1990), *mental models* (Senge, 1990), *organizational maps* (Argyris and Schön, 1978), or *organizational frames* (Bolman and Deal, 1991) to represent shared views of reality.

But the existence of such potent, persistent mind-sets may also be detrimental, filtering new information that might indicate the need to change. For instance, Kuhn determined that the most revolutionary scientific discoveries did not result from the sudden invention of new knowledge. In most cases, the relevant facts had been readily available for generations; however, they had been discounted or ignored because they conflicted with the old ways of looking at things. Instead, major leaps in scientific achievement most frequently occurred only after conventional assumptions were reexamined and old facts looked at in new ways. A similar process is recognized to occur with major innovations and breakthroughs in business, whether it is Hewlett-Packard's laser printer or Fred Smith's overnight delivery system.

For strategic change to occur, old mind-sets must be broken. But how does this normally occur? What causes organizations to ask deep, core questions about the nature of the business? Usually it is a crisis, especially a crisis that has the potential to threaten the health and survival of the firm. The frog, when immediately placed in boiling water, will jump out. Likewise, organizations learn how to change extremely rapidly when their future viability is felt to be at stake. Based on an examination of over a thousand articles on organizational change, Jack Zenger (1988) draws a similar conclusion: "As a rule [organizations] only change when pressured by some dramatic outside force. Corporations react to new technology, strong competition, or drastic changes in their markets" (p. 2). Zenger's examples include General Motors, Ford, Sears, Harley-Davidson, and the semiconductor industry. Consider the companies we feature in this book. For TRW, the catalyst was the uncertain future of the aerospace and defense industries after the end of the Cold War; for Royal Dutch/Shell, it was the volatility of the international petroleum industry; for Motorola, the Japanese-led quality breakthroughs in the electronic industry.

Learning through crisis allows for accelerated, revolutionary change. However, there is real danger in relying upon crisis to provide the impetus for meaningful change. Inherent in the crisis is, in most cases, an actual threat to the organization's survival. For every company that is able to engineer a turnaround during a crisis, many others do not survive. Moreover, at extremely high levels of crisis, the organization's learning mechanisms seem to shut down. Information becomes withheld and closely guarded. Personal well-being takes precedent over organizational transformation.

Certainly, external crises can trigger change by highlighting the gap between perception and reality, compelling organization members to scrutinize long-held assumptions and beliefs. But, in actuality, it is not the existence of an emergency that unfreezes organizations but the broad-based acceptance of the need to change and the ability to act based on that perception. This is a critical distinction. Two organizations faced with the same crisis might have very different perspectives about the need for change. One might be able to recognize the implications earlier than the other. One might be better equipped to handle the ambiguity and conflict that occurs when things are "up for grabs." And one might be better able to act in innovative and flexible ways, more quickly integrating changes across the organization.

Therefore, it is not the crisis itself that unfreezes organizations. It is the inherent readiness of organizations to change. Look at some corporations that have had recent trouble adapting, such as Pan Am and General Motors. These organizations were not surprised by sudden new events; in retrospect, they were aware of the forces in their industries compelling change for just as long as their competition, such as Delta and Honda. It is not that they were complacent; in many cases, they had engaged in ambitious efforts to meet changing customer expectations, address competitive challenges, and upgrade financial performance. However, compared to their competitors, they were less capable of taking advantage of crises as opportunities to change. Separating those firms that survive amid environmental turmoil from the competitors that do not are the relative states of readiness of the two firms.

Becoming Permanently Unfrozen:
The Importance of Strategic Readiness

Learning organizations question the traditional notion that fundamental change occurs only when companies are facing challenges to their immediate survival. Rather than waiting for crises to compel deep reexaminations of goals and plans, learning organizations attempt to stay permanently unfrozen by sustaining and intensifying states of heightened strategic readiness. Is it possible to unfreeze organizations intentionally? We believe strongly that it is.

A few years ago, we surveyed executives in several hundred companies to discover why certain organizations were able to plan and implement successful strategic change and others were not. To our surprise, the major determinant of success—alone explaining about 20 percent of the variation in the problems experienced from one company to the next—was the amount of effort devoted to readying organizations in advance for change. During follow-up interviews with twenty firms, we discovered that those companies most successful at producing fundamental strategic change had, in fact, engaged in a wide range of activities that had served to prepare the organizations in advance. We were amazed by the scope and intensity of the activities, which included the following:

- Many firms were embarked upon ambitious attempts to keep everyone, not just senior managers, aware of the external environment and the strategic position of the organization. In these businesses, communication took on a new sense of urgency and importance. In many cases, they sought to expand the direct and routine contact between members of the firm and customers, competitors, and other organizations. Moreover, they expanded people's understanding of the entire organization as a dynamic, interrelated system.
- Many organizations could best be described as learning communities. Systems were created to promote continuous learning by individuals, by teams, and by the organization as a whole. Work and learning were fully integrated.
- Many firms were purposefully building a wide range of

skills and approaches into the organization and creating flexible, continuously metamorphosing structures that possess the capability to redesign themselves to meet shifting business needs.

These firms were not merely engaging in activities aimed at helping the company change to meet a narrow, short-term challenge. Instead, they recognized that environmental uncertainty was a permanent condition. They accepted that change would be ongoing, not just something they did once and then stopped. They also acknowledged that it would not always be possible to plan in advance for a specific type of change, since environments are often inherently unpredictable. As a result, the following were common among organizations:

unfrozen

- Building a constant state of readiness had become recognized as a strategic imperative and embraced as a competitive weapon.
- Building strategic readiness involved not just temporary, one-time events but sustained, permanent activities, becoming part of the day-to-day operation of the business.
- Readiness efforts focused less on preparing to move in one specific direction or to adopt a single program and more on preparing for change in general.

In other words, more than just becoming temporarily unfrozen, these firms were attempting to stay permanently de-iced and ready to change by creating a deeply embedded capability to move quickly in new, unknown directions. They recognized that change is not something an organization does and is done with. Rather, change becomes something an organization *is*.

That is what we mean by strategic readiness. Traditionally, firms have turned to economic or financial capabilities, strategic or marketing capabilities, or technological capabilities to forge a unique and sustainable competitive advantage (Ulrich and Lake, 1990). Yet amid chaotic business conditions, constant strategic readiness may be the only source of a unique, sustainable competitive advantage. By building strategic readiness, organizations embrace the need to stay permanently unfrozen and ready to change. Such a "chronically unfrozen system," Karl Weick (1977) tells us, "may never have to redesign itself. With its steady diet of improvisation, its continual rearrangements of structure, its continual updating to meet changing realities, it may never need a major redesign" (p. 41).

In Part Three of this book we describe specific, concrete actions learning organizations take to develop their readiness to learn. Readiness activities can be divided into three categories: heightening strategic awareness, making learning a way of life, and continuously changing shape by becoming self-organizing systems.

Heightening Strategic Awareness

When crises threaten companies, everyone appreciates the need for strategic change—old mind-sets are challenged and, at least for a while, everything is in question. The threat to survival convinces everyone, not just a few executives, that the old ways of running the business are not working and that major change is demanded. Learning organizations, even without a crisis, attempt to create the same collective recognition of the crucial importance of strategic change. They demand increased awareness of the external business climate and of the need for continuous change in order to survive. When such alertness is combined with accurate, objective information on the organization's own performance, there is the possibility of creating a healthy dissatisfaction with the status quo that prevents companies from freezing to begin with. And by acquiring a broad, systemic understanding of the firm's processes, procedures, and structure, people are in the best position to appreciate the imperative of significant strategic change.

Making Learning a Way of Life

In learning organizations, work and learning are inseparably united. Each person is both teacher and student. The classroom is the shop floor, the computer terminal, or the customer's place of business. The subject is derived from the firms' most pressing strategic challenges. Knowledge is the primary product. And learning is the pivotal process. On the individual level, work and learning are synthesized, not relegated to off-the-job training and educational activities. On the team level, groups continually increase their capacity to learn together. On the organization level, a climate is created that nurtures continuous learning as a core competence. In addition, systems are established to allow the firm to tap the full range of its available knowledge, to bring that knowledge to bear on specific issues, and to apply the learning that occurs in one unit of the organization to problems in others.

Becoming Self-Organizing

Finally, there is a need for flexible, continuously shifting organizational structures designed to resemble continuously evolving living systems more than efficiently stable machines. By becoming self-organizing systems, learning organizations create the potential to act in creative, novel ways. They weave into the fabric of the organization a heterogeneous set of capabilities, perspectives, and approaches, exploiting their differences to spark innovative, unconventional thinking.

Examined individually, many of these readiness activities might not appear to be anything new. What is different is their intent, their intensity, and their impact on learning and strategic flexibility.

This ends our introduction to learning organizations—firms that approach strategic change as journeys of learning and that take steps to maintain a perpetual state of readiness for learning and change. Part Two takes a closer look at the strategic learning process through which learning organizations continuously plan, implement, and reflect upon their strategic directions.

ACCELERATING
STRATEGIC LEARNING

As described in Chapter One, many leading organizations are discovering that it takes more to be successful at strategic change than developing formal plans and executing them through fixed programs. Environments are too erratic and organizations too complex. Instead, plans are best when kept open and flexible, tested and refined through experimentation, and revised and adjusted as new information reveals itself.

The strategic learning cycle is the ongoing process through which learning organizations develop plans, implement plans, reflect, and adjust course as needed. The strategic learning cycle has three phases:

Continous Planning. In learning organizations, planning is an open process focused on taking quick action and preparing for quick review.

Improvised Implementation. In learning organizations, implementation is an evolving, experimental process designed to provide information for quick learning.

Deep Reflection. In learning organizations, reflection is built into all change efforts, aimed at questioning original assumptions and leading to broad and systemic learning in the organization.

The next three chapters will detail the types of actions learning organizations take to accelerate the strategic learning process.

4

Continuous Planning

How does planning in learning organizations differ from traditional strategic planning? Table 4.1 compares the traditional assumptions underlying strategic planning with those embraced by learning organizations.

Table 4.1. Traditional Versus Learning-Oriented Assumptions About Strategic Change.

Traditional Assumptions	Learning-Oriented Assumptions
Each strategic change is a new chapter in the firm's history. There is not much to be gained from looking backward.	Each strategic change is a part of a stream of change efforts. There is a great deal that can be learned from the past.
The future can be predicted. Therefore, plans need to anticipate forecasted changes.	The future is unpredictable. Planning needs to anticipate the possibility of a variety of futures.
A clear, consistent strategic vision will show us the path to the future.	The major value of a strategic vision is that it compels the firm to act and to learn.
Strategic change is best achieved through a detailed, formal, comprehensive implementation plan.	Strategic change is best achieved through triggering quick journeys of discovery focused on immediate business issues.

Planning in learning organizations is a continuous process that evolves from the questioning, refining, and modifying of existing plans. This chapter will outline four elements of the learning organization approach to strategic planning:

- Learning from the past
- Anticipating multiple possible futures
- Developing strategic visions and "re-visions"
- Establishing open, evolving plans focused on immediate business issues

Learning from the Past

Each organization, division, and department has its own past. Learning organizations consciously explore these histories, identifying benchmarks, time lines, problems, and successes, looking to derive a few central lessons that will apply to the immediate problem or issue at hand. Moreover, learning organizations are able to generalize from past problems and situations that, while apparently dissimilar to the current change, may offer useful insights into their ability to change.

Making History at Motorola

Starting in 1979, Motorola began its first attempts at quality improvement targeted to achieve what they called six sigma, a previously unheard-of level of excellence representing only 3.4 defects per million opportunities for error. In subsequent years, Motorola engaged in an ambitious and highly effective corporation-wide effort to improve quality—an effort that earned the company the prestigious Malcolm Baldrige National Quality Award. Now, fifteen years later, Motorola is approaching its six sigma target.

Recently, Motorola introduced the next iteration of corporation-wide strategic change efforts. One of them is the so-called software solution. In anticipation of marketplace demands, the software solution seeks to deliver to Motorola the same lead-

ership position in software as it currently possesses in hardware, thereby offering customers integrated solutions to their needs.

The senior management team coordinating the software solution process started with a careful study of six sigma, seeking insights that could be applied to this project. According to John Major, senior vice president and general manager of the Worldwide Systems Group, Motorola learned the importance of measurements to drive change efforts: "It is a common practice throughout Motorola to establish metrics which lead to internal competition and change. We also know that normalized measurement allows for corporate-wide change. Normalized measurement decreases the variance of individual business reasons for noncompliance with a change effort. A business can no longer say that the measurement does not apply to them" (1992).

In addition, the software solution team identified the most significant events in the history of six sigma, such as when a critical mass of managers understood and expressed support for the six sigma goal, when employees throughout the corporation did the same, when a few "islands of excellence" began to appear, and when formal operational reviews of the change effort were instituted. These key events were then used to set a time line for the software solution, with the target of achieving each milestone in half the time it took six sigma. John Major pointed out, "Not only were we to change the organization, but we had to change it more quickly than ever before. . . . We looked at our most recent corporate-wide change, our drive toward six sigma quality, and discovered it took us approximately fourteen years to achieve that quality. . . . We believed that decreasing the cycle time by 50 percent, seven years, will have significant impact for our organization and our customers" (1992).

However, Major is quick to point out that this schedule provides just a starting framework and must be adjusted as the software solution unfolds: "Part of the challenge of trying to change twice as fast is that the team does not yet know which portions of the time line can or must be expanded or contracted. Part of the team's learning is to figure it out."[1]

Motorola has learned invaluable lessons about strategic change from six sigma that will accelerate the software solution. These lessons were learned not through consultants' advice, nor by examining the best practices of other corporations, nor through seminars, books, or other external sources. The lessons were found in the organization itself, buried within its own rich history of change.

In fact, it is possible to portray an organization's past history as a series of macro-iterations of strategic learning. As described earlier, each strategic change is comprised of mini-iterations of learning, as the firm develops a plan of action, puts it into action, and reflects and adjusts course as time goes on. But on a broader scale, and from a longer time perspective, it is possible to see that each new strategic change represents an iteration of a larger, more encompassing strategic learning cycle.

For instance, we are familiar with an organization that over the past two decades has experienced major iterations of learning related to at least four aspects of quality improvement: zero defects (early 1970s), quality circles (late 1970s), total quality management (mid to late 1980s), and self-directed teams (early 1990s). Each of these eras of change represents a macro-iteration of strategic learning that is in turn made up of numerous mini-iterations.

As the organization moves from one macro-iteration to the next, there is an opportunity for learning. For instance, this company could learn a great deal about how best to introduce self-directed teams based upon its efforts with TQM, quality circles, and zero defects. However, opportunities for macro-learning derive not just from changes that are similar to each other, such as the various quality improvement cycles just listed. Companies can also learn a great deal from what on the surface appear as highly dissimilar types of changes. For instance, a firm seeking to radically overhaul its product line may derive critical insights from a diverse range of past change efforts, such as entering new markets, forming strategic alliances, introducing new technologies, and reorganizing.

What can be learned from old changes that would apply to new changes? There are two types of learning that can occur: (1) organization-specific insights into the firm's unique processes of change, and (2) general understandings about organizational change that might apply to almost any large, complex firm.

Organization-specific learning might relate to the following:

- Common roadblocks and problems
- The best methods of communication and involvement
- The probable manifestations of resistance
- The degree of openness to new ideas
- The ability to confront differences constructively

More general insights about change might include the following:

- It is important to keep expectations realistic.
- People will not support change for long if the company's reward system does not support it also.
- Changes are almost always more complex and take longer than imagined.
- New, unplanned events might occur that will require time and resources.
- The people who are affected by a change should be involved in planning the change.

Although it is important that an organization learn from past successes and mistakes, those lessons should not be automatically applied to future challenges. In fact, learning from past experience should teach us the danger of assuming that history will or should repeat itself.

How does a company learn from its past? By retrieving information regarding past history from the firm's collective memory. To do so, this information must have been previously saved for future retrieval. Many leading firms are beginning to develop formal methods of preserving their heritage of strategic change. These may include creating case narratives of previous change efforts, summarizing lessons learned from past experience, or developing historical records of organizational performance. In most cases, however, the only organizational documentation that exists is housed in individual memories, which, at best, store incomplete, biased, and often half-forgotten records of the past. In these cases, the best approach is to integrate the individual recollections into a composite consensus about what really happened, what worked and what did not, and what could have been done differently.

A word of caution: something surprising often happens when firms try to recapture their past histories of change. They tend to rewrite the past. When a company does so, it often reinforces the traditional mind-set about strategic change—that it started with some great master plan developed by a visionary leader and championed by maverick change agents. This make for a better story than admitting that they didn't know what they were doing, that they had to make some big mistakes before figuring it out, and that some of it just happened by chance and luck. Yet it is these uncomfortable revelations that often provide the most useful insights into the complexity of large-scale organizational change. They lead us to ask such key questions as, how could we have made mistakes earlier and learned from them more quickly?

Anticipating Multiple Possible Futures

As noted earlier, the distinction between planning in learning organizations and more traditional approaches to strategic planning is rooted in differing underlying assumptions about the predictability of the future. Strategic planning, as commonly practiced, presumes that future business conditions can be forecasted through the use of sophisticated environmental scanning techniques. The aim, then, is to detect weak, early signals of change and adapt to them, thereby becoming an agent in creating the future.

Learning organizations, in contrast, embrace the notion of the inherent unpredictability of complex, dynamic systems. They recognize that, given the chaotic nature of business conditions, companies will often be caught off guard by unforeseen events, even after paying close attention to environmental changes.

As a result, learning organizations recognize the need to anticipate futures that are not merely extensions of current trends. Instead, they consider the possibility that social, economic, and political forces will fundamentally transform the business landscape and that tomorrow may be nothing like today. They foresee times when competitors make startlingly aggressive moves no one expected. They envision futures in which new technologies have caused current systems and methods to become obsolete overnight. By anticipating the possibility of such apparently unlikely conditions, the firms will be better equipped to act in spontaneous and innovative ways when they inevitably face the unexpected.

If it is impossible to predict any one single future, how is it possible to plan? A process called *scenario planning* offers an approach. Through scenario planning, firms anticipate several different possible future scenarios and—instead of picking one as most likely, or even carving out a middle-ground position among the differing possibilities—plan for all of them at the same time. Scenario planning involves creating business strategies knowing that the deck is stacked with wild cards. To this end, Peter Schwartz, in *The Art of the Long View,* likens constructing scenarios to writing plays that contain complex, intertwining characters and surprising plot twists that leave the conclusion always uncertain: "One of the purposes of scenarios is to help you (or your managers) suspend disbelief in possible futures. To that end, you construct your plots as carefully as if you were in the theater. . . . You should design at least one alternative that frightens the management enough to think—but not so much that they shut down. Ask them to consider a future of shrinking markets, or even a hostile takeover. . . . Your goal is to select plot lines that lead to different choices for the original decision. What plots might make you do something different?" (1991, p. 145).

How does scenario planning work? The following is a typical approach to the process (Tenaglia and Noonan, 1992). A series of assumptions are developed to build a base-case scenario that presents the most likely future for the organization. Then a series of alternative scenarios, both positive and negative, are identified. Next, several acid-test scenarios are created—often three to five—that will most challenge the base assumptions of the business. These scenarios are used to spark the generation of creative business strategies that will (1) successfully manage the risks inherent in the scenarios and (2) maximize the firm's performance across the range of different possible futures.

Always Prepared for Change at
Southern California Edison

In the mid 1980s, Southern California Edison commissioned a study to evaluate its past twenty years of strategic planning. The reason? Its plans had been almost uniformly off-base. During that period, for example, plans had been made to increase the capacity to generate thirty-four thousand megawatts of power, when, as seen in retrospect, only nine thousand were actually needed. The review showed that there was nothing inherently wrong with the planning. The techniques were thorough and represented the best practices in strategic planning at the time. Each plan was based on the best information available. Instead, totally unforeseen, and totally unforeseeable, events had intervened to make each plan obsolete. The events were as follows:

- *Starting in the late 1960s, growing concern for the environment led to limitations on where sites could be built.*
- *The Arab oil embargo of 1973 caused a reduction in energy use that is still being felt. A similar event occurred in the Iranian crisis of 1979–1980.*
- *The Three Mile Island incident fueled antinuclear activities that threatened the nuclear power industry.*
- *The recession of the early 1980s slowed down growth overall and put several of Edison's major industrial customers out of business.*

The study recommended a fundamentally different approach to strategic planning. Adopting an always-be-prepared-for-change policy, Southern California Edison embraced the multiple-scenario planning methods.

First, several critical factors were identified, including rising fuel costs, economic growth, environmental constraints, technical innovations, and population growth. Then a base-case scenario was developed that took current trends and predicted their development over upcoming years. For example, the plan included a growth rate based on 2 percent demand. Then eleven alternative scenarios were generated. One postulated extremely high rates in fuel costs. Another, low economic growth. Another, an economic recession. And so on.

By examining these scenarios, Southern California Edison recognized that it needed to prepare itself for future demand that could fluctuate plus or minus five thousand megawatts from the base case per year. As a result, the new plans emphasized the ability to bring in additional reserves as needed, the capacity to bring plants on-line or take them off-line quickly, and measures to even out the spikes in demand. The scenario planning process now occurs on a two-year cycle with frequent updates in between. [2]

Developing Strategic Visions and "Re-Visions"

Vision has proven to be a crucial ingredient in successful change efforts. There are several examples in this book, from Motorola's vision of six sigma and the software solution to Micro Switch's drive for performance excellence. But is it futile and maybe even dangerous to establish a strategic vision when the business environment is chaotic and the future is unknowable? In *Managing the Unknowable,* Ralph Stacey makes a convincing case that strategic vision may be nothing more than a soothing fantasy: "If the future is inherently unpredictable, it follows that a single, organization-wide 'shared vision' of a future state must be impossible to formulate, unless we believe in mystic insight. Any such vision that managers put forward is then bound to be either a dangerous illusion or an interpretation of what has happened made with the benefit of hindsight" (1992, p. 13).

Yet we believe, when it comes to strategic vision, there is an inherent paradox. In fact, it is because the business future is unknowable that a shared vision is so essential as a driver of change. *In a learning organization, a vision provides the fuel that powers the collective journey of strategic learning.*

Early in this book, we employed an analogy based upon the

differences between two mountain ranges—one where the summit is always clearly visible, even at a vast distance; the other where the final peak reveals itself only during the last stage in an unfolding journey of discovery. This second mountain range, we asserted, is akin to the business landscape faced by most organizations as they enter the twenty-first century. It is in regard to this second mountain range that a vision is essential. If the peak can be seen, there is no reason to have a vision. But where the final destination cannot be seen, as in the second mountain range, it is important that those on the journey have a shared faith that there is a peak to be reached, that the peak is roughly as imagined, and that there is an urgent need to reach the peak.

In our view, the most effective vision is one that possesses the scope and power to mobilize a quick and ambitious journey of discovery. To do so, a vision must have scale. It must be grand enough to redefine what people aspire to and believe is achievable. The most potent vision often appeals to a higher sense of purpose, such as Steve Jobs's goal of putting a computer into every single person's hands. A vision must be uplifting and must demonstrate that the organization is not the servant of an uncontrollable environment but an active agent with power over its own destiny.

The original vision is less important than perpetual "revision." The most effective vision is continually evolving, transformed by the insights derived from the actions of discovery that the vision itself inspires. As such, a vision is best understood as emerging and evolving, shaped by the new perceptions gained through explorations of change. Tom Peters suggests that even the noble simplicities of "serving your customers" and "taking care of your people" can, in practice, degenerate into self-defeating mind-sets unless they are continuously redefined to fit current realities (Reimann and Ramanujam, 1992). For instance, according to Peters, IBM's vision of total customer satisfaction deteriorated into unquestioned loyalty to the wrong customer, and its commitment to people resulted in paternalistic overstaffing.

Moreover, an effective vision must become the shared psychological property of all members of the organization. So that this can happen, the vision must be seamlessly woven over time into the fabric of the organization. The failures of past change efforts have caused many organizations to become skeptical of impassioned calls to arms, no matter how eloquently delivered. In learning organizations, leaders recognize that a new vision will require time to take hold, as will the incorporation of the emerging vision into the firms' informal communication, reward, and information systems, as well as formal business plans. Also, a vision needs to be embodied in the personal and visible examples of management, integrating the vision into their normal activities. A stroll by Thomas J. Usher, president of USX Corporation, into the offices of the United Steelworker local to listen to the concerns of union leaders proclaims the corporation's new vision of management-labor partnership at U.S. Steel much more persuasively than any executive speech or program slogan (Hicks, 1992).

Searching for a Common Future: Search Conferences

Is it possible to involve the whole organization, customers, suppliers, and other key stakeholders in creating a collective vision of a shared future? A method called search conferences suggests that the answer is yes.

Search conferences were first proposed by Fred Emery and Eric Trist of the Tavistock Institute (1960). The process includes bringing together representatives from the "whole system" and together creating a shared vision of the future. Participants typically include a diagonal slice of employees, customers, suppliers, and union representatives. Conferences are several days in length and often include thirty to eighty participants, although search conferences in the hundreds are not unheard of.

According to Baburoglu and Garr (1992, p. 76), a typical search conference might be structured as follows:

Phase One: *Identify world trends.*
Phase Two: *Identify the desirable and probable trends that affect the organization as a whole or the specific problem or issue being examined.*
Phase Three: *Examine the evolution of the organization (or*

*the specific problem or issue), its history, and its
strengths and weaknesses.*
Phase Four: *Develop a future design of the organization (or
a plan to address the specific problem or issue).*
Phase Five: *Create strategies and action plans.*

*During each phase, small groups explore topics separately
and then reconvene to discover convergent and divergent thinking. The focus is on creating the future, not just solving yesterday's
problems. While differing perspectives are explored, the emphasis is upon locating common areas of agreement and building
from them. By the end of the conference, specific action plans are
developed with participants taking responsibility for making the
plans happen. After the conference, periodic follow-up sessions
are held to review progress and modify plans.*

In Discovering Common Ground *(1992), Marvin Weisbord
describes the application of search conferences to a wide variety
of settings, including:*

- *A health care center anticipating a future of reduced financ-
  ing, consolidation, shortages of skilled professionals, increased
  competition, and rising demands for services*
- *A recently struggling information systems company that now,
  apparently out of the woods, is seeking to establish a human
  resource strategy that will strengthen its competitive position*
- *A regional planning group in Canada that is striving to aid local
  economies by increasing entrepreneurial business developments*

Focusing on Immediate Business Issues

Once a broad collective vision is established, what is the best way
to trigger quick iterations of the strategic learning cycle? Rather
than waiting to develop fully detailed plans of action, learning
organizations seek to target the most pressing immediate business
issues that might help the firm move in the desired direction. There-

fore, as opposed to following traditional approaches to strategy implementation, learning organizations attempt to:

- Identify the most pressing, immediate, concrete business issues facing the organization
- Trigger quick action through ambitious short-term benchmarks
- Provide for quick learning through quick review

Driving Toward Significant Events at Motorola

We referred to Motorola's new "software solution" initiative earlier in this chapter. One of the key insights derived from looking at the preceding "six sigma" change effort was that it took many years to bring a sense of direction into focus. As a result, from the beginning, Motorola approached the software solution as an experiment in organizational learning. That is, rather than develop detailed strategies and action plans for achieving the software solution, Motorola established very general plans that could be the focus of initial learning activities.

As the first step, twenty-four senior vice presidents met at a Motorola University Senior Executive Program (SEP), supposedly to receive in-depth training on software. But that was only part of what occurred. Here is how the vice president and general manager of the Worldwide Systems Group, John Major, described what happened:

> *Many of us entered this three-day program prepared to experience what we had experienced in previous programs—intense exposure to a new subject area . . . and then back to the office where life would continue as usual. But, we were wrong. . . . As part of the SEP, we were also to engage in something called organizational learning—a process of learning by doing, reflecting upon what we have done, and making adjustments where necessary. . . . The SEP is not just for three days—that's the old paradigm called "learning"—it's for at least three years or as*

*long as it takes to get the job done. So while we are
a group of individuals with other primary
responsibilities—what you'd normally call a task
force—we're much more than a task force. We will
learn, experiment, document, implement, transfer
what we've learned about the process of leadership
for change to other groups with similar missions, and
most of all we'll do it faster than it's ever been done
before [1992].*

After the formal SEP program, members were divided into
five subteams, each assigned to lead the change effort in one
particular area as follows:

- Vision
- Management
- Process/metrics
- Tools/technology
- People

To integrate the activities of these subteams, a steering
committee comprising the five leaders of the subteams was established. Within this general framework, each team worked independently with the freedom to develop its own approach.

To accelerate the learning process, a calendar of short-term
significant events was created that would motivate and energize
teams toward action. In many cases, these events were arbitrarily
established with the sole purpose of causing quick iterations of
learning. And the best events were the most public ones. For
example, just three months after starting their work, teams were
asked to report on their progress at the Motorola officers' meeting. Another example related to the activities of "people champions" from throughout the company who volunteered to
investigate the software issues in their areas. After conducting
focus groups and producing written reports, the champions were
invited to make a presentation to George Fisher, then Motorola's
CEO, about their findings.[3]

Focusing on Concrete Issues

Learning organizations avoid centering change efforts around broad concepts like quality, participation, or world-class leadership. Instead, they identify a single issue or a small group of targeted issues that are immediately facing the organization. In many cases, these issues do not represent the ultimate destination of change efforts. Instead, they are used as vehicles to generate long-term learning. For instance, if the issue is quality, change efforts would focus on the most pressing quality issues relating to a specific product or service area. Keeping change efforts focused minimizes resistance at their early stages, allowing fragile efforts to incubate in their infancy and to take form as they mature.

Setting Ambitious Short-Term Benchmarks

To compel action, learning organizations often focus change efforts upon the achievement of a continuing series of ambitious, short-term benchmarks. Doing so establishes a sense of urgency that promotes quick action and, hopefully, fast learning. To build up speed, marathon runners employ a training technique called fartleks. Using fartleks, runners engage in a series of short bursts of running separated by brief pauses to catch their breaths. In one variation, during their routine long-distance practice runs, marathoners throw a tennis ball out in front, maybe twenty or thirty yards, then run after it, catching it after a single bounce. Then, after a brief passage of slower running, they repeat the process over and over again. By setting a series of ambitious short-term targets, marathoners are able to run long distances at increasing rates of speed.

Learning organizations seek to achieve similar results by establishing short-term targets and then sprinting after them. Continuous planning demands the creation of clear, results-oriented targets that establish reference points from which to plan future actions. Here is how one manager at TRW Space and Defense described the process: "We were always executing right on the heels of planning. When you left the room, there'd be a charter and a deadline. A sense of urgency was created because you don't have six months or a year but a month or two. There was a feeling that we couldn't wait for it. In any given week, there was always an extremely high level team review of the project."[4]

Planning for Quick Learning

Learning organizations do not wait for serious problems to arise before they examine progress and revise their plans as needed. From the very beginning, learning organizations establish frequent built-in checkpoints for reviewing progress, adjusting course, and expanding their efforts as progress is made. Quick reviews increase the opportunity for organization members to reconfirm their commitment to plans. They also make the process of change less overwhelming and threatening.

   This chapter covered the first phase of the strategic learning cycle—the continuous-planning process through which firms learn from their pasts, anticipate multiple possible futures, create shared visions, and establish evolving plans focused on immediate business issues. The next chapter details the second element of the strategic learning cycle: improvised implementation.

5

Improvised Implementation

In the Prologue, we briefly summarized the results of an important study conducted by Michael Beer, Russell Eisenstat, and Bert Spector (1990). This investigation, in our judgment, represents the most significant quantitative assessment of organizational change to date, measuring the success of initiatives in six large corporations (ranging from $4 billion to $10 billion in annual sales) engaged in revitalization efforts. Success was measured in two ways. First, after hundreds of interviews were conducted in each firm and a variety of corporate records were examined, researchers rated each firm on clearly defined criteria for measuring the spread of successful change in the corporation. These results were then corroborated through a standardized survey of members of the organizations being examined.

According to this study, the company ranked number one by both researchers and employers was General Products (a pseudonym).

Creating a Market for Change at General Products

In the late 1970s, General Products, a large, multi-billion-dollar, U.S.-based manufacturer dominated worldwide markets. But dis-

turbing signs were appearing. Its major European manufacturer, after achieving a major technological breakthrough, had launched a competitive product line that was rapidly taking General Products' market share. Moreover, the company's own production and marketing efforts seemed stagnant:

- Adversarial union-management relations (all plants were unionized) had threatened to stall any major alterations of processes and technologies.
- International marketing efforts were clearly less successful than domestic activities.
- New product development seemed tangled up in interfunctional fragmentation and miscommunication among engineers, scientists, and marketing.

As one of its first efforts to meet these challenges, General Products consolidated previously separate international and domestic marketing functions into a single "corporate" marketing department. The restructuring backfired. The international marketing department felt that it had been poised on the brink of several major successes in strengthening the firm's European presence and that the consolidation had pulled the rug out from under these initiatives. Moreover, to many, it was clearly evident that the new corporate marketing department was insensitive to the unique subtleties of individual international markets and products.

Within a few years, and after other false starts, General Products recognized that a fundamentally different approach to making change happen would be required. No longer could senior management simply devise a grand strategy to get them out of the mess and then oversee its implementation throughout the corporation. Instead, it became the senior managers' role to engineer a systemic process of organizational renewal that would rely upon experimentation, grass-roots innovation, and company-wide application of proven success strategies. As the vice president of marketing put it, they saw that their job was to "create a market for organization development" (Beer, Eisenstat, and Spector, 1990, p. 126).

Looking around the organization, management identified

several successful experiments and innovations that the corporation could build upon. A plant in Alabama had used high communication levels and employee involvement to reduce union-management tension and, as a result, had successfully instituted several significant innovations. Another plant had increased enthusiasm for a new product launched by sharing with employees the financial gains derived from the new product. A cross-functional team of engineers, scientists, and marketing managers had successfully implemented a new CAD/CAM system in order to accelerate the speed at which product prototypes could be offered to major customers. In addition, a nonunionized "greenfield" plant had been started in North Carolina to showcase the benefits of high employee involvement, the potential application of new technologies, and the possibility of radically streamlined production processes.

General Products then systematically engaged in a wide range of efforts to support these innovations, to encourage new change efforts, and to spread the changes throughout the corporation, as follows:

- Conferences were designed so managers could discuss their innovative practices with each other.
- The president and vice president took frequent trips to locations engaged in innovation.
- Meetings and corporate training sessions were held at the most innovative divisions.
- Performance and results were measured and communicated to demonstrate the success of innovative practices.
- Organization development consultants were made available to any division that wanted to use them, at no cost to the division.
- Lateral transfers of managers were increased significantly.
- The promotion system was changed to place greater emphasis on managers' innovative work in previous assignments.

Innovative activity gradually increased during the 1980s. In most cases, newer divisions showed change before older divisions, smaller ones before large ones, and geographically isolated *ones before those close to corporate headquarters. Yet, over time, the changes became clearly evident throughout the entire corporation. And the North Carolina plant continued to serve as the corporation's "beachhead" by breaking new performance records and serving as fertile ground for experimental efforts.*[1]

Unlike several of the other companies in the Beer, Eisenstat, and Spector study, General Products did not micro-manage the implementation process, developing highly specific schedules with tight time lines and strict accountabilities to ensure that changes were implemented as planned. Instead, General Products used a more improvisational approach to implementing strategic change (Perry, 1991). What strategies are used in improvising strategic change?

> *Encouraging Experimentation.* At early stages of a change, communicating support for spontaneous, grass-roots change initiatives throughout and establishing ad hoc structures to champion experimentation.
>
> *Directing Change in a Nondirective Fashion.* As change efforts begin to mature, sanctioning them without taking them over, quietly clearing away obstacles, and facilitating cross-fertilization.
>
> *Recognizing, Rewarding, and Institutionalizing Change.* After changes have begun to prove themselves, recognizing successes, rewarding achievements, and—at the right time—institutionalizing them with formal changes to structures, rewards, procedures, policies, and so on.

Encouraging Experimentation

The last chapter recommended that, as part of the strategic planning process, planners identify hot business issues and focus change activities upon experimental efforts tied to these issues. Yet, in many cases, the most important experiments are ones that develop on their own, without senior management intervention. Consultant

Elaine Biech calls this the "popcorn approach": "That's where you have all these little explosions and popcorn lies all over the place. It looks messy, like people are headed in different directions. And perhaps they are until someone can figure out what the new direction needs to be. You watch which way the kernels are flying and which ones end up the best and then move toward that" (Steinberg, 1992, p. 30).

In organizations where people are ready for change and share an understanding of the strategic direction, it is highly probable that change will begin to appear without the need for senior management to mandate it. In this way, all members of learning organizations are, to some degree, strategic planners. It is the leaders, however, who provide "the heat for the popcorn." And while leaders may feel that they are abdicating their responsibility to make change happen, they are still the ones who are cooking up the changes.

Spotting Grass-Roots Change Efforts

When experiments begin to pop up, they tend to surface at the firm's fringes, first becoming apparent in small, remote operations rather than in large, central ones (Beer, Eisenstat, and Spector, 1990). There are two reasons. First, there is often less pressure to follow corporate norms in geographically or structurally remote parts of the organization. Second, these units are often the first to feel the external pressures that are the impetus for strategic change. Because of their relative isolation, chances are that the results of these explorations will go unnoticed. As a consequence, leaders need to closely monitor all parts of the organization for individuals and units championing changes that are consistent with the firm's strategic direction.

Supporting Experiments

It is essential that those championing the emerging changes feel sanctioned and know that management is aware of and supportive of the initiatives being taken. This is best accomplished by reaffirming the overall strategic direction of the firm and promoting these efforts as examples of desirable activities and programs. By initially keeping experiments small, learning organizations can afford to encourage and support even duplicate and overlapping experiments; the competition between them can serve, in fact, to stimulate the flow of information.

Support can be created by featuring descriptions of change efforts in company newsletters, magazines, and videos. It can also be generated through programs and events specifically designed to promote change, such as friendly competitions among units and teams, award programs that reward experimentation, and showcase conferences in which proponents are given a chance to outline what they are doing. By providing visibility to experiments, even at very early stages, a subtle message is communicated: we value grass-roots change and those who lead it.

Another way to support experimentation is to allow mistakes. All learning involves some risk. Learning organizations increase risk taking and the willingness to take action under conditions of uncertainty by reducing the negative consequences associated with being wrong. Of course, this is easy to say but difficult to do. Being wrong too often does have potential long-term consequences—even cats have only nine lives. But learning organizations appreciate that it is possible to learn as much from unsuccessful actions as from successful ones—and sometimes much more.

Experiments can also be encouraged by minimizing expectations for short-term results. Control-oriented managers will quickly want to evaluate the payoffs. At early stages of change, such pressures can kill off experiments before they even get started.

Creating Ad Hoc Organizational Structures

Frequently, organizations introduce change by assigning responsibility to preexisting departments and delegating authority to individuals with closely aligned management responsibilities. Although there are many pressures to do so, managing change within the current organizational framework often does not work. Change by nature conflicts with the status quo. As a result, innovative, "out-of-the-box" changes are less likely to be incubated and developed if assigned to individuals who are responsible for daily business operations. They usually have many reasons for keeping things the way they are. Moreover, at early stages, changes often require significant investments of people, time, and resources. If these resources are not specifically dedicated to the change and if the change needs to compete with the daily demands of the business for resources, day-to-day operations will most often win out. Finally, at early stages, it may not be clear exactly what type of permanent changes to the organizational structure will be needed since it is not yet clear exactly what the nature of the change will be.

For all of these reasons, jump-starting change often requires such alternative organizational structures as cross-functional networks, task forces, project teams, and steering committees. Such temporary structures are able to circumvent the traditional, hierarchy-based communication patterns that often obstruct the nontraditional, lateral communication paths needed to stimulate successful transformation. They also provide legitimacy to change efforts and empower champions of change without dismantling the firm's current communication and power relationships.

In *The Learning Company* (1991), Pedler, Burgoyne, and Boydell liken the creation of these temporary structures to the erecting of scaffolding around a building:

> Scaffolding is something you erect around an existing structure so that the necessary building or rebuilding can be done. Scaffolding is a *temporary structure* that is not the change itself. In trying to bring about changes, it is very useful to have such a temporary structure to enable those involved in the change to have access to the familiar, and to hold things together until the change is completed. So you *don't* have to go straight from old to new, you can use temporary scaffolding around a difficult or contentious change that allows for the debate, discussion and revision of plans necessary before you commit yourselves irrevocably to a new system or structure [p. 82].

With change a constant, learning organizations are always under construction. Someplace and somewhere, scaffolding is always being put up or taken down.

Directing Change in a Nondirective Fashion

An improvisational approach to change can be threatening to many managers, conflicting with their conventional roles as leaders. Senge (1990) explains, "Our traditional views of leaders—as special people who set the direction, make the key decisions, and energize the troops—are deeply rooted in an individualistic and nonsystemic world view. . . . So long as such myths prevail, they reinforce a focus on short-term events and charismatic heroes rather than on systemic forces and collective learning. At its heart, the traditional view of leadership is based on assumptions of people's powerlessness, their lack of personal vision and inability to master the forces of change, deficits which can be remedied only by a few great leaders" (p. 340).

Senge then compares organizations to ocean liners, asking leaders, "What is your role?" Most see themselves as the captain or the navigator (p. 341). Yet Senge would argue that a more important and often neglected role is one of designer—the person who has engineered a powerful, flexible ship that can travel long distances and move in multiple directions.

Leaders in learning organizations build the structure and environment from which spontaneous change can emerge. Learning organizations ask leaders not to abdicate their responsibilities for strategic change but to assume an even more important role, facilitating the learning processes through which strategic change occurs.

Allowing Others to Determine the Specifics

While remaining deeply committed to making change happen, leaders must not mandate how the change should take place. It is essential that the ownership of change activities be assumed by individuals and units that are championing the initiatives. Consequently, leaders must avoid the tendency to introduce fixed programs or establish detailed plans, even when such approaches appear to provide the most effective and expedient route to the future.

Removing Barriers

One of the most powerful roles of leaders is to protect fledgling change efforts in their infancy, quietly and subtly removing impediments as they arise. Such support may include providing needed resources, such as time, money, or staffing. It may consist of neutralizing the influence of those in the organization who, possibly feeling threatened by the change, may attempt to thwart the initiatives. It may require altering or discarding restrictive procedures and policies. It may involve reducing structural roadblocks, such as narrow job descriptions or functional restrictions. Or it may consist of clearing away the smoke and dust that can cloud the organization's vision through simple reaffirmations of what is strategically important.

However, roadblocks should not be steamrolled over. In many cases, staffing, money, or time are real problems, with the new change efforts demanding resources committed to other priorities. In other cases, these issues may be symptoms of resistance, serving as surrogates for the real concerns people are experiencing. These underlying problems need to be revealed and discussed. When leaders remove the symptoms, provide new resources, clarify priorities, and encourage open dialogue, constructive exchanges may begin to occur and opportunities for learning may start to develop.

Encouraging Cross-Fertilization

As innovations take hold in one part of the firm, learning organizations provide means for disseminating achievements, spreading knowledge from one division to the next and from the fringes of the company to its core. They also freely spread news about their failures, knowing that organizations often learn more from experiments that do not work out than from those that do. Cross-fertilization can be achieved in many ways, such as by establishing forums, creating joint projects, and encouraging informal sharing of successes and problems. Implementation efforts are also enhanced by the sharing of insights with suppliers and customers, recognizing that the rate and quality of learning is dependent upon the firm's joint learning with key stakeholders.

Allowing Time and Space for Changes to Spread

The adoption of successful ideas and the quick rejection of failed approaches is facilitated by the availability of information from similar experiments. Consequently, there is a tendency to take what is successful in one part of the organization and to transplant it to the rest of the firm. However, it is important to recognize that, to some degree, each part of the organization must go through its own process of experimenting with and internalizing change. In fact, studies have shown that, when it comes to spreading change throughout an organization, it is often faster to "reinvent the wheel" (Beer, Eisenstat, and Spector, 1990, p. 92).

Regardless of how well a change has proven itself elsewhere in the company, each unit must go through what Colin Carnall (1986) calls a *coping cycle*. It has five stages, as follows:

> *Stage One: Denial.* This phase is characterized by a lack of acceptance of the need for change that results from an implied criticism of the unit's past performance. "Your old ways of doing things aren't working," the proposed change seems to suggest. In response, the unit targeted for change responds, "We have always done things this way, and it has worked in the past."
>
> *Stage Two: Defense.* After the specific nature of the change becomes apparent, there is a tendency for people to protect their territories and maintain the status quo. One form of defense is to attack the new change. And there will likely be a lot of ammunition at this stage because of the inevitable false starts and the unforeseen problems that often arise during the early phases of any change.
>
> *Stage Three: Discarding.* As the inevitability of the change becomes recognized, and as some initial signs of progress and improvement begin to be seen, people begin to let the past go and look to the future.

Stage Four: Adaptation. In this step, the unit slowly adapts to the change, modifying procedures, policies, structures, information flow, and so on. At the same time, the change modifies its form to fit the new environment.

Stage Five: Internalization. At this point, the new way of doing things is accepted as normal, and it is fully integrated into the unit.

The coping cycle is inevitable, and each organizational unit must go through it. Leaders need to provide time and space for people to come to grips with the change. To expedite the coping cycles, leaders can take steps to maintain the self-esteem of the unit, as well as to minimize the problems and difficulties that occur during the learning curve that happens with any new change.

Experimenting with Supplier Partnerships

A leading wholesale distribution company had over six hundred major suppliers, many of which drop-shipped their products directly to the end customer without the distributor touching the shipment. Faced with increasing competitive challenges and rising customer expectations for high-quality products delivered on time, the distributor identified improved supplier management as a major strategic issue. Yet the company did not know how to approach the problem. Direct inspection of shipments for defects was usually not feasible. Moreover, most suppliers resented any interference by the company, feeling in many ways that the distributor needed them more than they needed the distributor.

The first step was to create awareness of the importance of improved supplier management throughout the organization and to learn what leading firms in other industries were doing about the same issue. Next, as part of a three-year plan, supplier improvement was designated as a key strategic initiative. However, specific plans and programs were not mandated. Each product line had the freedom to try different approaches. The only requirement was that they had to do something that would signif-

icantly improve supplier performance and reduce the total number of suppliers within a three-year time frame.

Soon, a few experimental supplier improvement programs began to appear. One relied heavily on computerized linkages between top suppliers and the company. Another established an annual competition among suppliers based on a supplier performance report. A third developed supplier training programs and certification processes based on on-site audits of suppliers.

Senior management provided opportunities for each of the experimental efforts to explain their approaches and to be recognized for their achievements. And support also took the form of some additional financial and manpower allocations. Otherwise, it was hands-off. In the second year, the experiments began to look more and more similar as the key features of each were adopted by the others. Now, in the third year of the supplier improvement initiatives, measurement systems and formal accountabilities are being established. During these three years, supplier performance has improved 50 percent each year.

Tracking, Rewarding, and Institutionalizing Change

Much of improvised implementation is a matter of timing. For example, if formal support for a change is offered too early, or it comes too late, the initiative may not be successful.

Change efforts cannot succeed unless the organization fully supports the change. Leaders must exemplify the changes through their daily actions. People must be rewarded for performing in terms of new priorities that come with the change. Policies, procedures, and structure must also be supportive.

This is all true from a long-term perspective. But in reality, it is often best not to formalize changes at early stages. Why? First, high visibility and institutionalization may trigger resistance at a time when changes are least able to withstand opposition. Second, the gradual recognition and formalization of change serves to reward those experimental efforts that prove to be the best.

Therefore, rather than providing formal support and recognition of changes from the very beginning, learning organizations seek to shepherd new initiatives along by:

- Providing ongoing tracking of change activities as a feedback mechanism and to encourage further change
- Recognizing accomplishments and rewarding champions as changes prove successful
- Institutionalizing changes only after they are fully established

Again, it is a matter of timing. Just as there is risk in recognizing and institutionalizing change too soon, there is a danger in doing so too late.

Measuring Progress

Measurement is often a stumbling block. Objective, concrete data are essential for learning to take place. However, measurement can often be used to maintain traditional command-and-control forms of management, serving to demotivate advocates and derail new enterprises. For instance, time-honored ways of keeping score, such as rating short-term financial performance, can be used as ammunition to shoot down new ideas before they can get airborne. Many quality improvement efforts, even those that have been accorded the Baldrige Award, have been attacked on this basis (Garvin, 1991). In addition, well-intentioned goals and standards set when the full nature and complexity of change are still unknown can result in the establishment of unrealistic yardsticks against which to evaluate results.

Rather than focusing on control and accountability, measurements should emphasize progress and improvement. They should deal with a few of the most salient measures of the change, establish starting points, and chart movement over time. Moreover, not all measurements need to be quantitative and objective. Quick, informal assessments based upon subjective impressions of progress are often useful short-term evaluation methods. Such ongoing feedback drives the continuous improvement of implementation efforts.

Measuring the Speed of Learning at Analog Devices

Ray Stata (1989) of Analog Devices describes an innovative approach to tracking progress in quality improvement: measuring "half-lives" of improvement. For instance, the company tracked the number of times in which customers did not receive shipments on time. Each division then instituted a continuous improvement process designed to reduce the number of defects. After the process was in place for a year, the company assessed each division's half-life—the number of months that it took for each unit to reduce defects by half.

Analog has repeated this process for numerous other quality issues, including outgoing defect level, lead time, manufacturing cycle time, yield, and time to market. Surprisingly, regardless of the quality issue being attacked, half-lives seem to stay within a fairly narrow range of from six to twelve months. Through the use of half-lives, Analog has found a standardized measurement of the speed of learning as it identifies and remedies the causes of quality errors. Half-lives provided an objective basis from which to set ambitious improvement objectives. Using half-lives, it aimed to improve on-time delivery from 85 percent to 99.8 percent within five years. Moreover, once half-life baselines are established for each division, it is possible to set goals for reducing the learning cycle time. If a division is reducing quality problems in nine-month half-lives, it may seek to reduce the time to six-month half-lives. [2]

Recognizing and Rewarding Progress

As concrete, tangible progress becomes evident, such achievement needs to be recognized and rewarded in a variety of ways. The most powerful incentives are often the outcomes themselves (improved customer satisfaction, for example); the opportunity for meaningful involvement in exciting, high-impact projects; and the chance to acquire skills and capabilities that will last a career. Another powerful motivational factor is the increased personal visibility that comes from being part of many change efforts. Occasionally, tangible incentives (such as one-time bonuses) are needed to legitimize start-up undertakings. They can also provide an unmistakable signal to others that the organization is committed to change.

Institutionalizing Proven Change

Institutionalizing means making permanent changes to the organization's structure, rewards, procedures, policies, and information systems. Institutionalizing changes often brings broad resistance; as a result, it is best not to formalize any changes until they have taken hold on their own. Just as dangerous as institutionalizing too soon is not institutionalizing soon enough. After a change effort has begun to show signs of success, there is a danger of thinking that institutionalizing is unnecessary because informal, grass-roots approaches seem to be working so well. However, without formalizing the changes at the right time, the initiatives will continue to meet strong resistance and will inevitably fail.

Platforms for Change at Micro Switch

When Ray Alvarez took over Honeywell's Micro Switch division, he began sharing his vision of "performance excellence." In turn, the organization looked to Alvarez to clearly define what he meant by performance excellence and to provide a specific plan to achieve it. "People told me to give them a road map," Alvarez commented. "And to be honest, I had a road map in my mind, but I didn't want to give it to them. It would have stifled their creativity, and they have taken us far beyond where I would have taken us. I never would have expected this rate of change."

To encourage people to discover on their own what performance excellence meant on a daily basis in their own jobs, Micro Switch adopted a series of reward and recognition programs under the title of APEX (Achieving Performance Excel-

lence). One program provided for fifty-dollar Performance Awards that supervisors could give on the spot, $250-to-$500 Leadership Awards that were approved by directors, and $1,000-to-$3,000 General Manager's Awards approved by Alvarez. There is no limit on the number of awards that can be given each year.

The formal institutionalization of the changes has occurred through a series of "platforms for change." These included formal training systems, revamping tools and equipment, and adopting new technology. These formal systems were important because they showed people that Micro Switch was serious about performance excellence. "Putting your money where your mouth is," says Alvarez, "clearly communicates that this will not be another program that will go away in a few months."[3]

In this chapter, we discussed the second phase of the strategic learning cycle: improvised implementation. In the next chapter, we will cover the final stage: deep reflection.

6

Deep Reflection

At a recent strategic management conference, consultant and author Tom Peters debated Harvard professor Michael Porter (Reimann and Ramanujam, 1992). Their point of contention? Peters' assertion that business strategizing has become hopelessly outmoded. In a "world gone bonkers," Peters declared, no single business strategy, no matter how ingenious, no matter how well focused, can ensure a competitive edge for long. The preeminent problem for business today is excessive bureaucracy. Only by cleaning out the "gunk" from inside the corporation—in fact, only by radically overhauling our very notion of organizations—will corporations be able to mount the spontaneous, creative, strategic actions needed to deal with the messiness of the world. As an example, Peters proposed that IBM's CEO, John Akers, conduct a lottery in which each employee would randomly receive a number from one to nine. Those with numbers one and two would be immediately let go. Those with three to nine would each be divided into seven completely autonomous mini-IBMs. Now stripped down to a manageable size, the new, decentralized IBM would have a chance of making it in the crazy, high-tech computer manufacturing business in which it competes.

Porter disagreed. To him, Peters' argument violated the major underlying premise of strategic thinking, namely that "one must worship the environment, not worship the inside" (p. 38). All strategizing, Porter responded, must first start with an understanding of business conditions, not just a dismantling of the bureaucracy. Moreover, to Porter, action without underlying direction leaves organizations dangerously unfocused and incapable of meaningful collective action. "Do not throw the baby out with the bath water," Porter seemed to say. Yes, Porter conceded, strategic planning, as practiced in many companies, is often plagued by overanalysis and overly bureaucratic procedures. Yet, Porter asserted, strategic planning also provides a reservoir of tools and concepts that are indispensable for competitive survival in most organizations, including time-based competition, benchmarking, core competencies, strategic intent, value-based management, and strategic alliances.

In the debate, both Peters and Porter made valid points. It was a lively exchange, vigorously voiced and persuasively presented. But, in our view, the discussion was based upon an underlying fallacy. It assumed that organizational approaches to mounting strategic change can be positioned some place on a continuum between thinking and acting, between planning and implementing. Such an either-or distinction between thinking-planning and acting-implementing recalls the wisdom of Solomon. Solomon resolved a dispute between two women, each claiming that the same child was her own, by proposing to cut the child into two parts so each possible parent could have half. In much the same way, the Peters-Porter debate threatened to dissect the notion of strategic change into two lifeless halves.

From our perspective, thinking-planning and acting-implementing are inseparable. The purpose of a plan is to spark actions of discovery. The aim of implementation is to clarify strategic direction. Both are parts of the same whole process, the cycle of learning that occurs as companies attempt to mount strategic change. But the two phases—planning and implementing—are not enough to explain the strategic learning process. Something is missing. And that something is the process of reflection.

Reflection is the missing link between planning and implementation. Reflection has traditionally received little attention, either by strategic planning theorists or by practitioners. Planning has long been recognized as the heart of strategic change. Porter strongly supports that view. And over the last few decades, implementation has become increasingly recognized as critical. Peters is a convincing advocate of this position. In contrast, reflection is seldom discussed. Yet, once a learning-centered approach to strategic change is accepted, reflection must be embraced as an equal partner with planning and implementation. Through reflection, the sands of strategic change, the problems that companies encounter attempting to make plans happen, are transformed into pearls of learning. Once the critical contribution of reflection is accepted, a debate about the relative merits of planning and action becomes irrelevant.

In fact, reflection may represent the most important phase in the entire learning cycle. The other phases—planning and implementation—serve to provide the opportunity for learning but do not ensure that firms will learn from their experiences. It is during the process of reflection that learning actually occurs, as roadblocks are examined, causes uncovered, and solutions identified. These solutions are seen as provisional—not final answers but unfolding revelations that will be refined and modified through further exploration.

How do organizations build their capacity to reflect? Four steps appear essential:

- Providing frequent, ongoing opportunities for reflection throughout change efforts, even at very early stages
- Questioning underlying assumptions and searching for deep, systemic solutions to current problems
- Generalizing insights to other parts of the organization and to other issues, even those with little surface resemblance to the problem at hand
- Learning to learn by reflecting on the learning process itself and identifying ways to learn more quickly, deeply, and broadly in the future

Reflecting on Motorola's Software Solution

*Chapter Four described one of Motorola's experiments in orga-
nizational learning, the so-called software solution, a proposed
seven-year, corporation-wide learning process aimed at providing
Motorola with the same competitive advantage in software as it
currently enjoys in hardware. As part of Motorola's Senior Executive Program, five teams were created, each focused on one
element of the software solution. One of these teams, the vision
team, was charged with creating and communicating the software
vision for Motorola and its customers, providing an overarching
framework for the entire learning process.*

*As the vision team began its work, the team set out to
assemble available information about the corporation's different
markets, the role of software in these markets, competitive positions, and other strategic intelligence relevant to the software solution. The assumption was that the needed information would be
readily available, either in corporation-wide strategic intelligence
or in the long-range plans of company divisions. A date was set
for the team to meet again, assemble information, and take the
first pass at developing a vision.*

*When the team reconvened, it soon realized that the orig-
inal assumption was incorrect. Members were having difficulty
locating solid information about software markets and Motorola's
own software capabilities. The team then wrestled with a critical
question: How can we develop a vision of software without a full
understanding of the software elements of our markets and Motorola's own software capabilities in terms of market requirements? The team recommended that the original goal of developing a vision take a back seat to understanding the market,
obtaining a thorough self-education in software, analyzing Motorola's internal processes, and baselining its current software capabilities. Only after these steps were completed, the team came
to agree, could a vision be developed. As one member of the
team admitted, "This has been an important organizational learning experience for us. This is not to say that this team is stymied.*

*Just the opposite. The team is gaining strength. Our benchmark-
ing plans for [the next year] are quite aggressive and include
benchmarking a dozen companies, including some in Europe and
Japan" (Major, 1992). To represent the evolving nature of this
process, the vision team renamed itself the vision/marketing
team.¹*

Creating Ongoing Opportunities for Reflection

In most companies, reflection only occurs in one of two circumstances. The first is when a major problem arises during implementation that presents an obvious threat to the successful execution of
the strategy. Something is wrong—either with the plans themselves
or with how they are being implemented. The second is during a
periodic review of business plans. These are generally infrequent,
often occurring only annually or quarterly. Moreover, in most cases,
the purpose of these reviews is to judge whether plans are being
implemented on time as scheduled. The aim is accountability, not
introspection. The purpose is generally not to ask the hard questions that promote learning ("Are we headed in the right direction?" "What has surprised us?" "Were some of our original assumptions wrong?").

In learning organizations, attempts are made to provide frequent, ongoing opportunities for reflection. Learning organizations do not wait for problems to compel reevaluation. Reflection
is built into the implementation process.

At the start of a change effort, how soon should a firm stop
and examine how things are working? During the course of a
change process, how often should reflection occur? The answer to
both of these questions is: as soon as there is accurate information
available with which to judge progress and identify problems.
There must be some valid data available. That is why it is so important to set up good measurement systems at the beginning of all
change efforts.

However, there is a tendency to postpone reflection while
waiting for the accumulation of final results. For many change

efforts, it will be years until true outcomes are known. Strategic changes are, by their nature, often long-term processes. Competitive repositioning, entering new markets, investing in new technologies, forming new partnerships, changing basic product offerings—for all of these it will take many years to assess the outcomes. If an organization waits until the final results are in, it will be too late to make any meaningful adjustment of strategy.

Strategic changes are journeys. As with all journeys, it is best to change course, if required, as early as possible. Doing so will help avoid unnecessary backtracking. Minor adjustments early in a trip will make a major difference in the journey as a whole. Therefore, learning organizations seek to reflect early and often. They do so by looking for the first indications of progress and problems. Even at very early stages of a change effort, it is possible to quickly gather important information that will allow for reflection and adjustment of the course. Answers may be forthcoming to such questions as the following:

- Did customers first exposed to the new idea react as it was predicted they would?
- Did the first pilot project work as smoothly as hoped?
- Does new information conflict with what was known earlier?

Often, reflection is as simple as bringing people with a variety of differing perspectives together into the same room to help identify problems and discover solutions. The more perspectives, the greater likelihood that rapid learning will take place.

Questioning Assumptions and Searching for Systemic Solutions

The reflection process consists of exploring problems that occur during implementation and finding potential solutions. These solutions allow for the modification of plans, thus instigating another iteration of the learning cycle of planning-implementing-reflecting. Problems take a variety of forms. Some may represent major failures of the original plan. Others may be nothing more than the acknowledgment that there are always continuing opportunities for improvement. Another may be the discovery that intended changes no longer correspond with the latest information about customers, competitors, technologies, markets, and so on.

Regardless of the nature of the problem, the quality of the learning that derives from each rotation of the learning cycle is largely determined by how well the organization is able to identify and resolve the problem. Yet, in many cases, organizations avoid coming to grips with problems and then, after they do, they often fail to fully explore the causes and potential solutions.

There are many reasons why. All strategic change occurs in a political context in which the outcomes may alter the subtle power arrangements that exist within a firm. Strategic change deals with the most pressing issues facing the firm. There are often big winners and big losers, depending on how well the change did or did not work. As a result, when members of an organization come together to reflect on the successes and failures of strategic initiatives, there are often many other considerations that may influence how openly and effectively people explore the problems at hand and come to the best possible solutions. An individual's underlying questions may include the following:

- How can I protect myself and my allies against blame for any failures or setbacks?
- How can I maintain and possibly even increase my level of influence in the organization?
- How can I obtain proper credit and recognition for my contribution to the progress that has been made?

Such political issues often cause firms to avoid openly confronting problems, to misdiagnose them when they are dealt with, and then to contain the search for potential solutions to a narrow, limited series of causal factors. Each of these considerations can serve to inhibit learning. In many cases, it is only during subsequent iterations of the strategic learning cycle, when the true nature or impact of the problem is later revealed, that the firm is able to see that earlier opportunities for learning had been lost.

Games of Deception

In The Reflective Practitioner *(1983), Donald Schön analyzes the case of a new product failure in a large, U.S. consumer products firm. The company prided itself on its new product development capability, attributing its historical success to an exacting three-phase product-testing process. Before the firm launched any new products, they were mandated to undergo rigorous in-house laboratory testing, followed by extensive consumer panel tests, and, finally, several full-market tests. The product made it through the first two phases without a problem. Yet, during the market tests, evidence came back from the field suggesting that the product had the potential to catch on fire and to rust under normal use. At this point in the project, millions had been invested, and either one of these problems had the capacity to kill, or at least significantly postpone, the product launch. Management and technical reputations—not to mention careers—were on the line.*

These problems raised a tough question: why were these difficulties not uncovered during earlier testing, before millions were invested and when some possibly simple solutions could still be devised? Given the extent of management investment in making the change work, it is understandable that early signs of difficulty were first ignored and later misdiagnosed, attributing the failures to consumer misuse of the product. Management had been practicing what Schön called the "games of deception."

Finally when the company's responsibility for the problem could no longer be avoided and successful corrective action was taken, management was unable to openly reflect on what had led to the crisis since this would uncover their games of deception (p. 263).

This illustration serves to show how even highly sophisticated organizations—firms with leading-edge management and technical processes—can be subject to so-called games of deception that inhibit learning. These games help participants avoid dealing with problems, result in their misdiagnosis when they do come up, and limit open inquiry into their causes or solutions. For instance, if there is a problem that can be attributed to the isolated action of a single individual or to the failure of a solitary factor, then there is no need to raise more fundamental questions that may be more difficult for many of those in power to deal with. In fact, it is typical for companies to develop elaborate, fictitious explanations for failure that serve to show how the problem was a one-of-a-kind aberration, to attribute the failure to a single cause, and to document that all of the necessary corrective actions have been taken. Doing so minimizes the need to ask the hard questions that, while difficult to handle, provide opportunities for deeper learning.

In contrast, learning organizations seek to minimize these games of deception, seeking to take full advantage of every iteration through the learning cycle as an opportunity for learning. They do so by:

- Openly exploring differences and discussing the undiscussable
- Uncovering and challenging assumptions
- Searching beyond simple answers for systemic solutions

Exploring Different Viewpoints

When individuals convene to reflect on past performance, each person arrives possessing preconceived notions of what has worked, what has not, the causes of difficulties, and the best remedies. There is a tendency for reflective discussion to consist primarily of the advocacy of certain positions. Learning is maximized when advocacy is balanced with inquiry into others' perspectives (Argyris and Schön, 1978). Doing this effectively requires a suspension of disbelief in which one's own positions and perspectives are temporarily put to the side so that a free and open exploration of alternative viewpoints can be made. During an open exploration of perspectives, no issue or topic is felt to be undiscussable. Some of the most important breakthroughs in learning occur when taboo topics are raised and explored.

To openly explore differences requires new skills and abilities—most importantly that of being able to carry on dialogue. Senge (1990) summarizes the recent work of quantum physicist David Bohm, in which Bohm distinguishes between discussion and dialogue:

> Bohm points out that the word "discussion" has the same root as percussion and concussion. It suggests something like a "Ping-Pong game where we are hitting the ball back and forth between us." . . . By contrast with discussion, the word "dialogue" comes from the Greek *dialogos*. *Dia* means through. *Logos* means the word, or more broadly the meaning. Bohm suggests that the original meaning of dialogue was the "meaning passing or moving through . . . a free flow of meaning between people, in the sense of a stream that flows between two banks." In dialogue, Bohm contends, a group accesses a larger "pool of common meaning," which cannot be accessed individually [pp. 240–241].

In dialogue, individuals suspend original beliefs and assumptions and engage others as colleagues in the open pursuit of new meaning.

Challenging Assumptions

During the exploration of differences, learning organizations seek to uncover and challenge previous assumptions. All plans for change are founded on suppositions, often unstated, about the causes of past difficulties and the characteristics of successful change. Such prevailing mind-sets are often strongly and deeply held. In learning organizations, old assumptions are quickly identified, directly confronted, and openly explored. Learning is maximized when problems are examined not just "with the grain" (accepting the existing assumptions) but "across the grain" (questioning the original premises) (Lessem, 1991, p. 33). Therefore, members of learning organizations make special efforts to separate facts from assumptions. When presenting a certain point of view, individuals make sure to explain how they arrived at the conclusion, inviting others to offer disconfirming information and competing perspectives. Learning is most productive, Senge (1990, p. 199) asserts, when "everyone makes his or her thinking explicit and subject to public examination. This creates an atmosphere of genuine vulnerability. No one is hiding the evidence or reasoning behind his views—advancing them without making them open to scrutiny. . . . I might say, 'Here is my view and here is how I have arrived at it. How does it sound to you?' " In many cases, a major breakthrough in learning occurs with the recognition that assumptions have been treated as facts.

Searching for Systemic Solutions

Learning organizations do not take problems at their face value. Organizations are complex systems. Any problem evidenced in one part of the organization is likely to be intricately entangled with a host of other issues.

The foundation for the notion of strategic learning is that most organizational problems can be traced back to multifaceted, deeply rooted causes. The immediate surface problems are presumed to be symptomatic of underlying issues. To address these root problems, organizations look for systemic solutions, rather than ones that address only an immediate limited-scope difficulty.

But the value of efforts that are less broadly targeted should not be discounted. In the search for systemic solutions, even narrowly focused change efforts—initiatives aimed at a single issue or engaged in by only one part of the organization—have the capability to acquire knowledge that can be broadly applied. They often produce insights into the basic structures, processes, information systems, procedures, policies, management practices, and norms of the organization.

It is this search for systemic solutions that characterizes what we call systemic (Level Two) learning and what Argyris and Schön (1978) label *double-loop learning*. The idea is simple. Take a problem. Identify its potential causes. Then rather than stopping there, treat the causes as the problem, and identify the causes of the new problem. And continue this process as far as it is possible and feasible to go, much like peeling back the layers of an onion.

For example, a company's total quality program is failing after a year. Evidence suggests that the cause is a lack of middle-management support. It would be possible to stop here (that would be Level One or *single-loop learning*) and identify ways to ensure that support, such as by increasing the communication, training, or involvement of middle managers. This would be dealing with the immediate symptom of the problem. But there is an opportunity for further learning if the lack of middle-management support is then treated as the problem. A full exploration of underlying causes might include an examination of the organization's reward system, structure, goals, processes, and other factors. Without addressing these deeper issues, any attempt to address management's lack of support for the total quality effort may offer short-lived and limited improvements. It is likely that a year later the company would be meeting again, still wondering why middle management is sabotaging the quality program.

Dialogue as a Matter of Survival

Streaking across the bright blue, early morning sky above the Saudi Arabian desert, the U.S. Air Force AWACS (Airborne Warning and Control System) reconnaissance planes—with their revolving, mushroom-shaped radar devices on top—searched for enemy aircraft. As if a knife had sliced the sky into three pieces, the radar screen was divided into three clearly defined sectors, with bright red dotted lines marking where one sector ended and the next began. An aircrew comprising several weapons directors controlled and coordinated the movements of the numerous defense aircraft. Each weapons director, with several aircraft assigned to his or her control, was responsible for one of three sectors. After hundreds of hours of training, each weapons director knew his or her responsibility clearly—to defend his or her assigned sector. With each person taking responsibility for a specific sector, the air space could be best defended.

For several hours, each weapons director monitored his or her assigned sector with little sign of enemy planes. But suddenly, five unidentified aircraft appeared as blips on the screen, cutting diagonally across the sectors on the screen. Then the aircraft veered in seemingly unpredictable, random ways. A plane would approach the line separating two sectors, and, almost as if it knew where the line was drawn on the radar screen, the plane would turn in the opposite direction. For a few minutes, one of the weapons directors would have three or four enemy aircraft in his sector. Then, just as quickly as they appeared, they disappeared, crossing over into another weapons director's sector.

The following conversation occurred among three weapons directors—Sam, Bill, and Mark—as they decided how to respond to the enemy attack:

Sam: *You've got another guy coming into your lane, here.*

Bill: *I've got everybody in my lane. Do you have anybody?*

Sam: *No I don't. Well, let's see.*

Bill: *Hey, hey, somebody needs to get this guy here.*

Mark to Sam: *You've got a plane in the area. Why don't you send him over?*

Sam: *I can't do it at the moment. I'm oversaturated.*

Mark to Sam: *Damn it, we've got to cover all three lanes, not just our own. Everybody's getting shot down. I'll cover you.*

Sam: *There's just nothing I can do.*

Mark to Sam: *Okay, never mind. I'll get him. I'm sending number twenty-one through your lane. Cover me.*

This scenario did not actually occur over the skies of Saudi Arabia. It was part of a simulation for AWACS aircrews conducted in 1990, many of whom would soon be in combat in the Persian Gulf war in situations very close to the one described. The simulation was designed to pose a difficult dilemma for the weapons directors. On one hand, should they maintain control and respon-

sibility for their assigned sectors (and not worry about the other sectors) as they had been taught? Or should they temporarily merge with the other weapons directors and share responsibility for all three sectors, at times leaving their own sectors temporarily unprotected while they assist the others?

In a breakthrough study of organizational learning, Tom Broersma (1992) discovered that the number-one factor influencing the success of one aircrew versus another was the degree of open dialogue. He found that the more the aircrews engaged in open dialogue about the validity of the original defense plan, the higher the aircrew's "kill ratio" (how many aircraft were shot down by U.S. crews compared to those shot down by the enemy). For all seven aircrews studied, when they engaged in dialogue 69 percent of the time, the kill ratio was three to one or higher. Broersma's study shows that open dialogue is clearly a matter of survival as well as success.[2]

Generalizing to Other Issues and Parts of the Organization

After discovering potential solutions to a problem, it is tempting to stop there, since the immediate impetus for learning has been addressed. Yet learning organizations recognize that knowledge created in any one context can often be applied elsewhere. After identifying problems, reflecting, and discovering possible solutions, learning organizations are mindful to stop and ask how what they have learned may be applicable elsewhere, to other problems, to other parts of the organization struggling with similar issues.

It is a surprise to most organizations that they encounter strikingly similar problems from one change effort to the next. In such cases, the knowledge derived from one type of change might be equally applicable to another. Moreover, learning can also be generalized from one part of the firm to another. Since organizations are complex, interrelated systems, it is likely that the new knowledge has sweeping application, even to an organizational unit with a remote relationship to the situation at hand. Yet a careful balance must be maintained here, since differing organizational units will, to some degree, need to make their own mistakes and discover their own solutions. In many cases, however, this process can be accelerated by embracing the learning encountered by other divisions of the same organization.

Yet it is often difficult to transfer to others the intimate, personal knowledge one gains from experience. Ikujiro Nonaka, of Tokyo's Hitotsubashi University, calls this *tacit knowledge* (1991). It represents the implicit and unspoken insights of the best performers. Yet for knowledge to be transferred, it must be expressed, made explicit. It is a truism in sports to say that the best performers are rarely the most successful coaches and managers. Although they possess the most developed tacit knowledge of the sport, they have not developed the skill to make the knowledge explicit so it can be communicated and embraced by others. According to Nonaka, making personal knowledge available to others in the organization is a central ingredient in the success of the top Japanese corporations. To make tacit learning explicit, Nonaka asserts, it is necessary "to express the inexpressible" through metaphors and models (p. 99).

For example, Honda used gambling as a metaphor to capture the knowledge that innovation requires risk taking. After experiencing great success with the Civic in the 1970s, Honda was finding in the early 1980s that its product development efforts were becoming focused on replicating this success by coming up with better and cheaper Civics. Yet, after reflecting on several different new product successes and failures, a few key managers recognized that new product development was not unlike gambling. There were no sure bets. And success could only occur if risks were taken and products were brought out that were substantially different from those already on the market. This analogy gradually became encoded in a motto, Let's Gamble, which served to guide much of Honda's new product development efforts of the 1980s and 1990s, continually prodding Honda to develop innovative automotive designs rather than just to produce better Civics. Through the use of the gambling metaphor, Honda has been able to continually remember an important lesson from its early years—that successful product development requires risk—rather than needing to learn the lesson over and over again.[3]

Learning to Learn

There is one final component of the reflection phase of the learning cycle: the act of reflecting on the learning process itself in an attempt to identify ways in which it can be improved. The aim is to discover methods that will increase the speed, depth, and breadth of learning in the organization. Doing so represents the highest form of organizational learning—learning how to learn. Why is learning to learn the pinnacle of organizational learning? Because it enhances the strategic capability of the organization, allowing the firm to be more successful, not just with the current strategic change, but with the vast array of changes it will face in the future.

How does learning to learn work? At the culmination of each iteration of the learning cycle, learning organizations stop and ask, "How could we have learned more quickly, deeply, and broadly?" Here is how Argyris and Schön (1978) describe the process, which they refer to as *deutero-learning:* "When an organization engages in deutero-learning, its members . . . reflect on and inquire into previous episodes of organizational learning, or failure to learn. They discover what they did that facilitated or inhibited learning, they invent new strategies for learning, they produce these strategies, and they evaluate and generalize what they have produced" (p. 27). This process should focus on each of the three phases of the learning cycle (planning-implementation-reflection). For each phase, it includes taking a hard look at what worked and what did not work, posing the question, Could we have learned more and faster if we had done X rather than Y?

Take the example of a division of a leading international high technology corporation that recently experienced difficulties with a major new product launch. After looking back and examining how it originally planned the change, the division discovered that it had a tendency to develop specific, concrete strategic goals at very early stages and to hold people accountable for meeting these original projections.

After going over the plans, the same division was surprised to find out that it actually discouraged creative experimentation and grass-roots change efforts by expecting short-term measurable outcomes. People had been afraid to make mistakes. Instead, to encourage creativity and experimentation, there should have been little pressure for immediate results, only for getting out there and trying some things to see what works and what does not. After studying the reflection process, the division came to accept that it avoided dealing with implementation difficulties until they turn into full-scale, "stop everything" emergencies. It vowed to pause frequently in the future to assess how things were going and catch problems at their earliest possible stages.

One of the most powerful forms of learning to learn takes place not after major failures but after significant breakthroughs. With the perspicacity derived from new insight, it is possible to turn a glance over the shoulder to previous iterations and ask, Why didn't we discover this earlier? Why did we avoid confronting the real issues for so long? Why did we need to go through so much pain before asking the tough questions? Such inquiry leads to profound discoveries, such as uncovering the built-in defense mechanisms that protect old mind-sets from open examination. Or, after finally discovering systemic (Level Two) solutions to long-standing problems, obtaining for the first time a clear view of the self-obscuring mechanisms that kept the company focused on symptomatic (Level One) solutions during earlier iterations. Or, after finally seeing that "the emperor has no clothes" and coming to grips with the inaccuracy of original assumptions, recognizing ways that these false premises could have been confronted much earlier.

Obviously, learning how to learn has a powerful impact on an organization's capacity to plan and mount strategic change. Yet learning to learn is often neglected. Why? There are several reasons. First, many organizations are too busy urgently putting out the fires caused by long-ignored implementation problems to invest the time needed to examine the learning process itself. Second, asking questions about the firm's learning processes initially feels unnatural and awkward. In most traditionally run companies, it simply is not done. At the end of a meeting focused on confronting implementation problems, it is not typical for someone to stop and say, "Now, before we leave today, what can we learn here that might help us to avoid such problems in the future?" Such questions appear esoteric and remote, until the pervasive, potent impact of learning to

learn is experienced firsthand and becomes accepted as an integrated
and essential part of strategic change.

✳   In fact, the ability to assess and improve learning may represent the single most important defining characteristic of successful
organizations. As a result, learning organizations establish a climate
in which learning to learn becomes natural; in which reflection
occurs early and often, thereby minimizing the crisis atmosphere that
prohibits inquiry into learning processes; in which blame fixing is
avoided, thus allowing the freedom to openly explore the complex
processes of organizational learning. Gradually, learning organizations come to feel comfortable with the process and to appreciate the
immense strategic value of continually and consciously enhancing
the firm's learning capacity. Soon, it seems unnatural *not* to stop and
ask, How could we have learned this earlier?

Is Micro Switch a Learning Organization?

*Previous chapters have explored several initiatives that Honey-
well's Micro Switch division has engaged in under Ray Alvarez's
leadership to increase the firm's learning capacity. Personally convinced that a great deal of progress had been made, Alvarez recently sought to see if others felt the same way. To do so, he
surveyed fifty opinion leaders in the organization and asked them,
"To what degree is Micro Switch a learning organization, relentlessly pursuing new knowledge, and applying the new knowledge
in the pursuit of continuous improvement?"*

*The responses were initially both surprising and disappoint-
ing to Alvarez. Over half of the people said that they did not think
that Micro Switch was a learning organization or that they were
not sure. "To be honest," Alvarez reflected, "I have to say that I
am still in the process of digesting it, of accepting that even after
five years of relentless pursuit the jury is still out on whether
Micro Switch is a learning organization."*

*Since then, the initially perplexing feedback has been used
to spark a dialogue about what it means to be a learning organization and to what degree Micro Switch possesses these charac-*

teristics. *In these conversations, a recurring theme has emerged. The firm has not been able to take advantage of some opportunities for learning because people have been afraid to admit mistakes. While Alvarez was well aware that this had been a historical problem for Micro Switch, he felt that the fear issue had dissipated. "They talked about the fear factor, the fear of change, the fear of failures. I would have thought that we had gotten over that. I think that is one of the big things I learned this year." Now, the Micro Switch team is exploring ways to overcome "the fear factor" as a means of accelerating learning.*

By stopping for a minute and reflecting on whether the firm was a learning organization, Micro Switch learned how to learn. In the process, it demonstrated many of the most important features of learning organizations: the willingness to be vulnerable, the openness to exploring differences, the good judgment to check assumptions, the tenacity to search for systemic solutions, and the sagacity to recognize that they did not have all of the answers. It proved that the real answer to the question appears to be, yes, Micro Switch is a learning organization.[4]

With this chapter, we end our discussion of the three-phase cycle of strategic learning: continuous planning, improvised implementation, and deep reflection. We now turn to steps organizations take to build their readiness to learn.

PART THREE

BUILDING
STRATEGIC READINESS

As we described in Chapter Three, any organization's ability to learn is determined, in large part, by its strategic readiness. The next three chapters will identify specific actions learning organizations take to enhance that readiness.

To explore what is meant by strategic readiness, let us use as a model the policy of commercial airlines regarding seat belts. On most flights, except during takeoffs and landings, the seat belt sign remains off. The assumption is that weather conditions will be fairly calm and predictable. During these conditions, the pilot will be able to scan the horizon (if not visually, then through the use of instruments), detect any mounting signs of turbulence, and have sufficient time to warn the passengers to return to their seats and buckle up.

On other flights, weather conditions are such that it is not always possible to forecast future conditions and to respond to them quickly. As a result, the pilot requires that passengers remain in their seats with belts buckled, in a state of readiness for any surprise turbulence.

Today, most organizations exist in turbulent business environments that require all members of the firm to be buckled up permanently and prepared for anything. No longer can the pilots of the firm merely keep an eye on the horizon, vigilantly watching for any early signs of business turbulence, and then prepare the organization for change once a danger presents itself. By the time plans are developed and implemented successfully, it may be too late.

Learning organizations, firms that build strategic readiness as a permanent part of their nature, take their competitive flights with seat belts always secure. Strategic readiness represents a state of permanent, organization-wide preparedness for large-scale, systemic change. Learning organizations exist in a constant state of readiness, preparing not only for small-scale changes but for change in general. They stay attuned to their environments, are willing to question their fundamental ways of doing business, and are aware of themselves as complex, interrelated systems.

Actions that learning organizations take to enhance strategic readiness include the following:

> *Heightening Strategic Awareness.* Many firms are engaged in ambitious attempts to keep everyone, not just senior managers, aware of external environments and the strategic position of the organizations. In these businesses, communication takes on a new sense of urgency and importance. In many cases, they seek to expand the direct and routine contact between members of the firm and customers, competitors, and other organizations. Moreover, they develop people's understanding of the entire organization as a dynamic, interrelated system.
>
> *Making Learning a Way of Life.* These organizations can best be described as learning communities. Systems are created to promote continuous learning by individuals, by teams, and by the organization as a whole. Work and learning are fully integrated.
>
> *Becoming Self-Organizing.* These firms are purposefully building a wide range of skills and approaches into the organization and increasing their ability to create flexible, continuously shifting structures to reflect the continuous learning of the organization.

7

Heighten Strategic Awareness: Understand the Need for Continuous Learning

To learn in deep and fundamental ways, organizations must discuss the undiscussable, question the unquestionable, and explore the unexplorable (Argyris and Schön, 1978). To do so, everyone in the organization must fully understand and be aware of the need for a radical transformation of the business. To build this elevated awareness of the need for change, learning organizations engage in a sweeping series of readiness activities, including:

- Heightening awareness of the environmental forces that have the potential to affect the organization
- Generating healthy dissatisfaction with the status quo
- Developing awareness of the organization as a complex system

Heightening Environmental Awareness

Recently, we attended a company social event sponsored by a firm with which we had just begun to work. Such an informal setting would, we hoped, afford insights into those elusive aspects of the organization that might not be grasped during our brief, structured visits. At our table were twelve individuals spanning various divisions and layers of the company.

111

While engaged in a conversation with the people sitting near us, we overheard the following discussion at the far end of the table:

"Did you hear that [the firm's major competitor] was cutting prices by 10 percent the beginning of next month?" the first voice asked.

"No, I hadn't," responded the second person. "But I'm not surprised. They have been trying to buy market share for quite some time now. They don't have any other choice, given how we're dominating the high-end market. And did you see the last customer survey? We're just blowing them away. But, I don't see how they can hold on for long. Their margins have to be suffering."

After a few minutes, we turned to see who was talking, expecting the voices to belong to senior managers. To our surprise, they did not. Instead, we discovered that we had been eavesdropping on the conversation of two customer service representatives. For the next ten or fifteen minutes, they continued discussing business conditions, untangling competitive positions as perceptively and passionately as many senior managers (maybe more so).

The heightened awareness of and concern for the corporation's business environment demonstrated by the two individuals in this conversation (given that others share such insight) should supply a significant competitive advantage for this organization. Why? To explain, let us discuss the psychological concept of *attention,* the process through which individuals align senses to certain stimuli in their environment and ignore others. Attention is a necessary prerequisite to learning. At an individual level, if a person is not attending to relevant stimuli in his or her personal environment (whether it is the voice of a teacher, the red light at the corner, or the altered behavior of a troubled family member), he or she is incapable of learning. The same is true for organizations. If organizations are not attending to certain stimuli, they also will be unable to learn.

Traditionally, most individuals in organizations attend primarily to internal stimuli. For managers, these stimuli include a fairly limited set of business performance indicators, such as measurements of financial health, productivity, efficiency, and quality. For frontline employees, the scope is even more restricted, dealing with the day-to-day details of immediate job responsibilities.

If companies are going to be able to anticipate and adapt to environmental changes, they must attend to their external environments. Yet, in most cases, the collective attention of organizations is directed internally, not externally. For example, look at your own organization. What percentage of the new information that each person receives each day relates to the internal operation of your organization? In comparison, consider what percentage is from or about customers, competition, suppliers, and industry trends? Based upon our experience, if more than 10 percent of the daily informational input is external in nature, your organization is a rare exception.

No wonder many companies have trouble mobilizing for strategic change. Such change aims to reposition organizations in dynamic environments; yet, in terms of the day-to-day realities experienced by most members of most firms, external environments barely exist. Reality is restricted to what happens within the firm's four walls. The outside world and the strategic issues it generates are treated as incidental and irrelevant for most people.

Learning organizations seek to direct the collective attention of enterprises to both external and internal factors equally, forging complete and holistic understandings of organizational realities. External and internal considerations are not viewed as distinct, but as two sides of the same coin. Moreover, strategic awareness is not limited to a few select senior managers. And by broadening the base of heightened sensitivity to the company's strategic position, learning organizations preclude the need for actual survival-threatening crises to emerge before they recognize that significant change is required.

Learning from and About Environments

Most organizations engage in systematic attempts to obtain information about their environments by conducting market research (focus groups, customer surveys, and so on), by gathering intelligence, by tracking industry trends, and by following broader social and economic forces. In most cases, these data-gathering activities are treated as special projects, completed outside the realm of normal operations, planned by senior management, and delegated to either internal or external market research specialists. Typically, information retrieved through this process is tightly held by senior executives. Widespread communication of the information is frequently felt to be irrelevant or distracting to most members of the organization. Moreover, there is often a concern that the more widely intelligence information is shared, the greater the likelihood that it could find its way into competitors' hands.

As do most other companies, learning organizations actively scan and gather information from their environments. But there are a few notable differences in learning organizations (Table 7.1).

In learning organizations, environmental scanning and intelligence gathering are no longer limited to periodically conducted, formally planned projects. Instead, these functions are integrated into the daily operation of the firm, where "staying close to customers" and "understanding the market" become routine components of job responsibilities and company operations. Similarly, learning organizations understand that informal sources often deliver the best environmental intelligence; therefore, they seek to capture insights derived from routine interchanges with

Table 7.1. Environmental Scanning and Information Gathering: Traditional Versus Learning-Oriented Approaches.

Traditional Approaches	Learning-Oriented Approaches
Information gathering occurs through periodic projects.	Information gathering occurs as an ongoing process.
Formal sources are preferred.	Informal origins of information are valued as much as formal sources.
Information is closely held.	Information is widely distributed.
The main emphasis is upon acquiring new information.	There is an equal focus upon using information available within the firm and obtaining new information.
Information is treated as discrete "snapshots" of data.	Information is analyzed and integrated to reveal emerging patterns.

clients, competitors, suppliers, and other external contacts. Learning organizations also appreciate that firms have vast amounts of tacit knowledge just waiting to be tapped and used. As a result, they establish methods of linking and synthesizing preexisting information. Moreover, learning organizations encourage all members to share responsibility for obtaining and disseminating insights about shifting business conditions. To do so, firms keep individuals aware of organizational needs in certain categories of information and reward contributions to intelligence-gathering efforts.

Building Awareness Through Employee Communication

Communicating to employees about business conditions is nothing new. Most companies have attempted to keep employees apprised of customer needs, competitor moves, and industry trends, at least to some degree, through employee communication programs. But when we speak of the need to increase the awareness of the environment, we are referring to activities that, while in some ways similar to traditional employee communication are different in purpose, scope, and intensity. The aim of traditional employee communication is to enhance morale, a function that is often a human resource department's responsibility and to some degree seen as an employee benefit. Employee communication represents something the organization does—although with the best of intentions—often somewhat condescendingly. When there is a downturn, budgets for employee communication are often the first to be slashed. In addition, the scope of most employee communication programs is rather limited, consisting of occasional newsletters, video presentations, and management speeches. Information tends to be limited to favorable views of the organization, highlighting major accomplishments and showcasing significant events. When employee communication is limited to presenting only positive, self-affirming images of the company, it serves to maintain the status quo.

In learning organizations, the purpose of employee communication has changed, and the stakes have been raised. What is at risk is the very survival of firms. The aim is to recast entire organizations as integrated systems, poised, vigilant, and ready to alter their fundamental ways of doing business. All employees are periodically provided updates on strategic information previously the province of only top executives, including facts related to:

- Competitive pressures (major competitors, their key strengths and weaknesses, potential threats, possible new opportunities, and so on)
- Customer needs (major customers and their changing expectations, for example)
- Industry trends (such as technologies, new markets, and the effects of economic and social trends on the industry)

In learning organizations, the communication of relevant external information becomes a daily event, transmitted through a variety of formal and informal means. New technologies—like voice mail, electronic mail, and computer networks—are explored as potential vehicles for communication. Common methods include:

- Holding periodic (annual, quarterly, monthly) updates on past business performance and future business goals
- Tracking and communicating a small, pivotal set of company performance indicators, such as customer satisfaction measurements, quality standards, market information, and financial performance data
- Conducting benchmarking studies and communicating their results throughout the organization

Benchmarking is powerful, not only because it provides useful insights into other organizations but also because it helps companies to see how they compare to these firms. Benchmarking can redefine for firms what they view as feasible and what is not. It can also help previously self-satisfied organizations recognize the need for improvement.

Competitor and Customer Awareness at Micro Switch

Ray Alvarez, vice president and general manager of Honeywell's Micro Switch division, describes an innovative series of company-

wide events designed to increase employee awareness of competitive pressures and customer expectations: "We began with a competitive awareness month where we spent a whole month and a lot of departmental meeting time exposing employees to who our principal competitors are, on what basis they are competing with us, and what it is going to take to win against them."

This month-long learning experience concluded with a dramatic event designed to bring home the competitive pressures facing the organization. "Everyone was invited to come to work dressed up in battle gear," Alvarez recounts, "and they dressed me up as General MacArthur. Others arrived wearing football gear, military gear, and firefighter gear." Micro Switch applied a similar approach to the issue of customer awareness, with the aim of urging employees to think about how the company helps its customers compete.[1]

Communication at Federal Express

Few companies devote as much effort to heightening employee awareness of business conditions as does Federal Express. Through a sixty-person, ten-million-dollar investment, the company runs FXTV, the largest corporate television network. A five-to seven-minute news broadcast is transmitted daily via satellite to over twelve hundred locations where employees can stop at lunch rooms or conferences and receive the latest update on company performance (stock prices, volume, and service performance) and view prerecorded news features that might report on competitive moves, marketplace shifts, and changing expectations of customers. Often broadcasts are done in a call-in talk show format. According to CEO Fred Smith, the FXTV investment has paid for itself many times over.

Equally ambitious is Federal Express's daily communication of the company's service performance through its Service Quality Index (SQI), which is compiled through a computerized tracking system called COSMOS. Each service failure receives a point value based on research that has correlated each failure to its impact upon customer satisfaction. For instance, if a shipment is delivered late but on the same day, one point is deducted. If the shipment *arrives on the wrong day, that is a five-point penalty. And if the shipment is lost or damaged, that is ten points. People pay special attention to the SQI, since performance evaluations and bonuses are directly tied to the final scores.* [2]

Building Awareness Through Direct Interaction with the Environment

Employee communication is an important way to create an awareness of external business conditions. Yet there is an even more powerful method: providing every employee with ongoing opportunities for direct, intimate contact with customers, suppliers, competitors, and others outside the company.

The advantages are several. Direct contact provides an undiluted and immediate understanding of environmental reality rather than the distilled and remote version most often presented in company communication vehicles. No longer are environmental changes represented by sterile numerical projections or abstract conceptualizations; instead, for each member of the organization, they become vivid and take on personal meaning. In addition, this method turns entire organizations into vast receptors of environmental information. While personal external contact has traditionally been limited to top management, in learning organizations, everyone takes on the role of a *boundary spanner*. As a boundary spanner, each member of the organization is expected, encouraged, and enabled to have direct contact with customers, suppliers, and others outside the boundary of the firm. Methods for direct contact include:

- Encouraging all employees to take responsibility for assisting with environmental scanning and information gathering
- Promoting direct customer-employee contact on a routine basis, especially for those behind the scenes
- Expanding the participation of organization members at trade shows and conferences
- Establishing strategic alliances with suppliers, customers, and

competitors with direct peer-to-peer contact between the two organizations

---

Employees as Customer Satisfaction Researchers

Three years ago, a leading wholesale distribution company conducted its first customer satisfaction survey, employing the services of a market research firm. Since then, the firm has administered the same survey internally, using frontline employees as researchers. Volunteers are recruited from throughout the company. After receiving a half day of training in phone survey methods, the individuals make three days of telephone calls to customers. The company's aim is to ensure that every employee will have a chance to participate in the survey because of the increased insights they frequently gain regarding customer requirements. In turn, the callers are involved in summarizing the results, presenting the findings to the rest of the company, and establishing plans for improvement based upon the results.

One recent year, the company needed more people to make calls than were available at the time. So a group of retirees was invited to come back and work with the current employees making the calls. An added benefit, according to the company's market research director, was that "because the retirees had both a long-term perspective of the company, as well as some distance from day-to-day operations, they could see things we just couldn't see. They helped us recognize how much progress had been made over recent years. But, at the same time, they helped us clearly confront our current shortcomings."

Throughout the year, individuals are encouraged to communicate information they come by through their routine contacts with customers and suppliers; some often use the company's voice mail system to broadcast detailed accounts of these exchanges to colleagues and senior management. In addition, all employees are invited to spend a day each year visiting local customers, asking for feedback on the firm's performance, and seeking suggestions for areas to improve.

Inquiry Centers: Permanent War
Rooms at General Motors

When one looks for an example of an organization that failed to see what was going on around it when many others did, General Motors is a popular choice. In the 1980s, both Ford and Chrysler responded to the Japanese challenge by streamlining themselves and moving from "mass manufacturing" to "lean manufacturing." GM, on the other hand, was big and rich enough that it was temporarily buffered from the full impact of the changes in consumer demand and the threats of competitor moves. But times have changed. In 1992, GM reported a $23.5 billion loss with only a 34.9 percent U.S. market share (compared to over 50 percent a few decades ago).

"Can GM be saved?" Fortune asks. "Certainly. But that will require something revolutionary for GM: adapting quickly not only to its own altered circumstances but also to those of the world around it" (Taylor, 1992, p. 61). One method being experimented with is inquiry centers—rooms where people can go at any time, any day, to obtain the latest external intelligence, to meet and exchange insights, and to brainstorm and creatively explore different options. While inquiry centers are physical locations, maybe more importantly they represent a new philosophical orientation for GM. Vincent Barabba, GM's executive director for market research and planning, explains, "The inquiry center describes a particular way of learning about the marketplace and using the resultant knowledge. While the term 'center' denotes an organizational unit, it can be as much an attitude, ethic, or creed as it as formal entity" (Barabba and Zaltman, 1991, p. 5).

The idea behind inquiry centers is that "the voice of the market" does not belong just to senior executives or market research departments. Instead, it must be made accessible to every person in the company every day. In that way, inquiry centers are permanent war rooms.[3]

Generating Healthy Dissatisfaction

To be ready for strategic change, organizations need to do more than create a heightened awareness of the environment. No matter how well people understand the external forces necessitating change, day-to-day realities may blur any recognition of the need for that change. In many cases, the basic components of businesses—their structures, procedures, communication patterns, and power arrangements—are so firmly entrenched that to even think about changing them is taboo.

As a result, learning organizations seek to gently but persistently question the basic assumptions that underlie their businesses. They maintain a healthy sense of discontent with the status quo, recognizing that what produced success yesterday will not ensure survival tomorrow and perceiving the current situation to be both FUBAR ("fouled up beyond all recognition") and EGBAR ("everything is going to be all right") at the same time (Vaill, 1989, p. 79). "Every organization needs to prepare for the abandonment of everything it does," Peter Drucker (1992) counsels. "Managers have to learn to ask every few years of every process, every product, every procedure, every policy: 'If we did not do this already, would we go into it now knowing what we now know?' . . . Organizations increasingly will need to *plan* abandonment rather than try to prolong the life of a successful product, policy, or practice" (p. 97).

One approach to generating healthy dissatisfaction is to paint as realistic and detailed a picture of the firm's current situation as possible. Just as learning organizations devote considerable energy toward building an awareness of the external environment, they also work to establish an equally clear understanding of what is happening within the firm itself. As a result, threats and uncertainties are communicated as fully and forcefully as are achievements and goals. Creating a combined understanding of both environmental pressures and organizational realities produces organizations able to appreciate the necessity for strategic change.

Another approach is to compare the organization to some existing external standards of high performance and excellence. Many companies are impressed by their quality improvement efforts until they take a hard look at themselves using the Malcolm

Baldrige National Quality Award criteria or the ISO 9000 guidelines, the European standards for quality improvement processes. Many organizations are comfortable with their own leadership positions until they conduct competitive benchmarking studies that show what "best in class" and "world class" really look like. To Robert Galvin, the former CEO of Motorola, the passion for achieving unparalleled levels of quality starts "by first pointing out that it is possible to run the four-minute mile" ("A Conversation . . . ," 1992, p. 62).

Another method of creating healthy dissatisfaction is to break up patterns and do the unexpected. Organizations have rhythms—regular procedural and structural patterns—that must not become too firmly entrenched. Leaders need to come down on the offbeat now and then, challenging the bureaucratic habits of companies by changing established procedures, reorganizing company structures, and altering key policies and processes. The approaches can be simple, like disrupting normal procedures of meetings—doing without an agenda, if there normally is one; changing the setting, location, and schedule; or inviting different participants (Pedler, Burgoyne, and Boydell, 1991). The methods can be more dramatic, such as shifting the responsibilities and roles of key players. For instance, a company feeling that it was becoming stagnant rotated its senior management in a game of musical chairs. The result? In their new positions, managers were able to bring a renewed energy, creativity, and perspective to the task, while still being able to tap the knowledge and expertise of the "old" managers.

Creating Healthy Dissatisfaction
at Honeywell Micro Switch

When Ray Alvarez took over responsibility for Honeywell's Micro Switch division, his first impression was that the company had become stagnant, limiting capital investment and losing its reputation for quality, integrity, and dedicated people. Yet, within the organization, there was a feeling that nothing needed to be changed and that any failures were only temporary setbacks.

Many executives pointed to an ambitious quality improvement program that had been instituted several years earlier and listed many significant achievements that occurred as a result of this program. They even thought that the Malcolm Baldrige National Quality Award might be within reach.

Within this context, Alvarez set out to establish a healthy dissatisfaction with how things were going with the company. Some key managers were replaced, and the senior staff was reorganized. A change-agent team of fifty key managers—the Eagle Visionaries—was formed and began an ongoing series of change management workshops. There were competitive-awareness weeks, as well as a series of informal briefings on business conditions designed to increase awareness of the need to change. Employee communication efforts were expanded, with quarterly business updates designed to focus everybody's attention on company performance.

In addition, the services of a leading international quality improvement consulting firm were engaged to assess the company against the Malcolm Baldrige National Quality Award criteria. The report was critical, suggesting that while the company was going through the motions of quality improvement it possessed two major weaknesses. First, the quality improvement process was neither directly integrated with the strategic planning process of the firm nor directly related to customer requirements. Second, personal, active leadership was limited to the top layer of management and was still not being demonstrated by middle managers. In addition, the strong emotional appeals used to build employee commitment to quality improvement, combined with several notable early successes, had engendered a short-lived state of euphoria that may not be sustainable. According to the consultant's report, "employees' excitement and enthusiasm grew because of many visible signs of progress and positive change. Early successes were communicated widely . . . creating unrealistic expectations about the difficulty, timing, and impact of the change process."

This discovery propelled the organization to engage in a series of ambitious new efforts, and today the firm is recognized as the number one supplier by several top customers. Despite the *progress, the company continues to maintain a healthy dissatisfaction while at the same time celebrating its accomplishments.*[4]

Nurturing Systems Thinking

But understanding the external business environment and creating dissatisfaction are not sufficient. People must also become aware of how things work within the organization. What power a company would achieve if every member of an organization was a systems thinker. What a competitive edge would be attained if each person saw the immediate task in terms of the larger context; acted in independent and creative ways to serve the organization's higher purpose; appreciated the complex influences of their actions upon other parts of the organization; and looked for deep, double-loop, systemic solutions to the daily problems and roadblocks encountered on the job.

According to Senge, the recognition of the critical importance of systems thinking is the cornerstone of learning organizations: "Systems thinking is a discipline for seeing wholes. It is a framework for seeing interrelationships rather than things, for seeing patterns of change rather than static 'snapshots.' It is a set of general principles—distilled over the course of the twentieth century, spanning fields as diverse as the physical and social sciences, engineering, and management. It is also a set of specific tools and techniques. . . . And systems thinking is a sensibility—for the subtle interconnectedness that gives living systems their unique character" (Senge, 1990, pp. 68–69).

Systems thinking, with its holistic and interdependent understanding of organizations, exists in stark contrast to bureaucratic and mechanistic understandings of organizations.

Given the inherent complexity of organizational systems, change processes might not always produce intended results. Senge (1990, pp. 57–67) outlines the following "laws of the fifth discipline" which detail the difficulty of intentional change in complex systems:

1. Today's problems come from yesterday's "solutions."
2. The harder you push, the harder the system pushes back.
3. Behavior grows better before it grows worse.
4. The easy way out usually leads back in.
5. The cure can be worse than the disease.
6. Faster is slower.
7. Cause and effect are not closely related in time and space.
8. Small changes can produce big results—but the areas of highest leverage are often the least obvious.
9. You can have your cake and eat it, too—but not at once.
10. Dividing an elephant in half does not produce two small elephants.
11. There is no blame.

According to Senge, change efforts that do not embrace the entire organization as a complex system are doomed to fail.

A Learning System That Doesn't Learn

Could it be that the U.S. educational system is a "learning system that doesn't learn?" The Consortium on Productivity in the Schools believes so. As evidence, the head of the Consortium, Sue Berryman, notes that "the core technology of K-12 [kindergarten through high school] has not improved in this century." Bringing together some of the best minds from business management, public finance, economics, health care, and education, the Consortium is seeking answers to such questions as:

- *Why the educational reform efforts of the last decade are not producing significant improvements in student learning and performance*
- *Why significant research breakthroughs in education often do not find their way into practice in the schools*
- *Why the best practices pioneered by one school or district infrequently spread throughout the school system*

- *Why schools, even when they achieve improvements, find it difficult to sustain the initiatives over time*

Simply stated, "productive change just isn't happening as fast as it should." So says G. Carl Ball, the chairman of Geo. J. Ball, Inc., and the president of the Ball Foundation, the Consortium's sponsor.

What makes the Consortium unique is its systems approach to looking at education. Most attempts at educational reform focus upon a single aspect of the educational system (such as funding, teaching methods, student motivation, family influences, and social-economic factors). "Single bullet reforms are almost inevitable," Berryman concludes, "because American educators and policy makers have no shared understanding of K-12 as a system. Thus we have no basis for selecting one versus another reform and move restlessly among them." The result is a confusing and contradictory crazy quilt of reforms at federal, state, district, and school levels. In fact, there is some evidence that current reform efforts are, in some cases, making things worse, not better.

In contrast, Berryman believes that any fundamental answers must be found by studying the system as a whole: "Too often we've picked up pieces when it is the system that needs to be talked about. Until we try to understand that, and how the pieces go together, it's hard to know how to make changes. . . . It isn't one thing, it's all of them." To take a systematic look at American education, the Consortium is going through the following steps:

Current Situation	Step
1. *Limited understanding of how parts of the system interact.*	*Map the education system to determine how it really functions.*
2. *Changing educational processes without addressing the system's ability to learn.*	*Identify the learning disabilities of the education system and design recommendations to correct those dysfunctions.*
3. *Limited knowledge of*	*Identify performance standards*

	what changes behaviors of those engaged in the system.	*and incentives and, perhaps most importantly, the underlying norms and values.*
4.	*Limited knowledge of productivity improvements in other sectors.*	*Study connections between productivity issues in education, health care, business, and other fields.*
5.	*Constantly supporting activity that does not lead to change.*	*Work with stakeholders to create a national framework that connects activities at all levels of education and government to yield change.*

Working with Innovation Associates, a consulting firm of which Peter Senge was one of the initial founders, the Consortium is creating an "as is" map of the educational system. Still in its early stages of development, the map explores the complex interactions among various parts of the education system as a means of finding out where the key leverage points are for future improvement efforts. For example, one part of the emerging map is a diagram called "Shifting the Burden" (Figure 7.1), which illustrates the unintended consequences of external interventions into school systems.

Jennifer Kemeny of Innovation Associates explains:

When there is external intervention in a system, it tends to have a couple of effects. One, it takes away the opportunity for the local area to learn how to do it itself. Relying upon outside forces to resolve problems often has side effects that cause the local area to actually be less able to do what it needs to do. As school boards, states, and other governing bodies put more and more restrictions, directions, or imperatives on how schools are to operate, teachers find themselves with less and less freedom to make local decisions themselves. In fact, they lose the skills needed to learn how to work effectively together independently, and it is usually disempowering. The

Figure 7.1. Shifting the Burden.

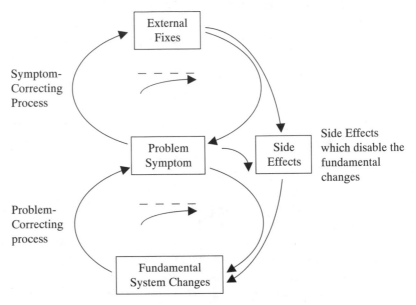

When faced with a problem symptom, it is easy and quick to
correct it from the outside. This not only takes the pressure
off of internal changes, it may create side effects which
disable the corrective capacity of the system, necessitating
more external intervention.

result of "shifting the burden" is that over time you
actually get more dependent on external intervention as you cripple the system. This is not just about
teachers. Shifting the burden occurs at all levels. For
instance, we are concerned that children in the
school system are victims of shifting the burden because the responsibility for education lies solely with
their teachers and administrators, not with the children themselves. As a result, they never learn to be
responsible either for their learning outcomes or for
developing the skills required to become lifelong
learners. One wonders if this lack of responsibility
for their educational outcomes transfers to their lack

of responsibility for other life outcomes, perhaps contributing to the development of self-destructive adolescent behavior.[5]

How does a firm create an army of systems thinkers? Much of what we have talked about so far in this chapter goes a long way toward building a foundation for systems thinking. Heightened awareness of external environments is a first prerequisite. The ambitious steps that many organizations are taking to keep members aware of what is going on outside help to instill a new and broader conception of the firm as a complex system interrelating with a dynamic set of external factors. Thus it is also important to engender a broader understanding of organizations themselves—their processes, their structures, and their current performance—in order to promote system thinking.

Developing Systems Thinking Through Simulations

In The Fifth Discipline, *Peter Senge (1990) describes the use of simulated microworlds, which build the capacity for systems thinking. A microworld is "a microcosm of reality where it is safe to play," allowing for individuals and teams to experience the long-term, unintended consequences of their actions (p. 314). Although the name may be foreign, Senge affirms that microworlds are not anything new. They are reflected in children's play activities, in survival exercises that executives use in wilderness team building, and in role-playing scenarios often found in supervisory training.*

Senge describes how, with the help of computer technology, microworlds are able to assume a new potency in their ability to simulate the dynamic complexity of organizational systems. For instance, microworlds were used as part of a two-day planning retreat for a computer manufacturing company that had just established a highly aggressive sales objective. The plan was based on two assumptions: (1) sales could be increased by hiring a large number of new sales representatives, and (2) the per-person productivity of the sales force would remain constant over the next several years. The simulation allowed the management team to experience the long-term consequences of their actions, discovering inherent fallacies in these assumptions. New sales representatives, it was shown, would not be as immediately productive as the current sales force. Moreover, current sales representatives would lose productivity while working to bring the new people up to speed. Therefore, the ambitious sales objectives would not be achieved using this plan. As a result of the microworld exercise, more realistic sales projections were made from the beginning, and the management team anticipated many problems without having to experience them first.

By creating a heightened awareness of business conditions, by generating healthy dissatisfaction with the status quo, and by expanding capacities for strategic thinking, learning organizations increase their readiness to learn and to change. The next chapter explores another way that learning organizations build their strategic readiness: by making learning a way of life.

8

Make Learning a Way of Life: Enhance Individual, Team, and Organizational Learning

In this chapter, we examine how learning organizations work to make learning a part of everyday life. In learning organizations, work and learning are inseparably linked. A defining element of learning organizations is the transformation of firms into institutions that promote continuous, day-in, day-out learning—individually, in teams, and throughout the whole community.

On-Line Learning at College Pro

College Pro Painters was founded in 1971 by Greig Clark, a recent college graduate who wanted to employ the knowledge he gained from his experience running his own painting company while he was a college student and make a business out of it. Therefore, from the beginning, the concept of College Pro Painters was based on the idea of taking knowledge gained from experience, capturing it, and disseminating it to others quickly and effectively. And today, that is quite a task. With many features of a virtual corporation, College Pro's small nucleus of about 120 full-time employees swells to over 6,000 each summer, becoming the largest residential painting company in the world.

College Pro is now led by CEO Steve Rogers, an early Col-lege Pro painter and manager. Under Steve's leadership, College Pro has expanded rapidly into almost all of the United States and diversified to include a year-round painting division, Certa Pro. College Pro itself is now a member of the FirstService Corporation family of companies headed up by CEO Jay Hennick. FirstService Corporation is the second largest residential services company in North America.

From the beginning, it was clear that the success of the business depended on the ability of the company to recruit, train the franchisees, market the services, and deliver the services to the customer. College Pro to this day employs a mixture of class-room and on-the-job training for franchise managers to teach them the needed mix of business, people management, and tech-nical painting skills. Indeed, in its Philadelphia area operations, it has built a full-scale street front of houses in a warehouse in order to be able to train franchise managers in painting during the win-ter. Smaller versions of the indoor house front exist across the company.

To fuel this growth, the company's general managers—those who have hired and supervised the franchise managers—have been the critical link in enabling the business and as a result have been a central focus for training. Since the general manager is the leader of franchise preparation and management, general managers need to be competent in a wide range of skills. These skills include recruiting and selection, painting and estimating, budgeting and finances, facilitating adult learning in and out of the classroom, goal setting and review, coaching, conflict resolution, problem solving, and situational leadership, to name a few.

During the early years some of the skills were taught to general managers in seminars by external trainers, but College Pro realized that, in many cases, classroom training had limited im-pact. Simply, it lacked follow-up and means to measure the use of the skills on the job. In one early experiment to overcome this problem, classroom training was supplemented by a simulation and feedback process that closely approximated the real-life situa-tions general managers faced on the job. For example, for estimat-ing and selling skills, a house was set up as a test site and a "trainer" would act as the customer. Rookie managers would then make an estimating call on the house, with their general managers present to observe and give coaching. The rookie would go around the house, and after the estimate, he would sell the customer/trainer on the estimate. After the selling session, the general manager gave feedback to the rookie manager on his estimating and selling skills. Then the trainer gave the general manager feedback on his coaching skills. This simulation-based approach represented a major step in moving learning from the classroom to real-time learning in real situations. It was soon applied to a wide range of other skills, and detailed competency models were developed to specifically outline how specific skills would be applied in the context of College Pro.

Still, College Pro wondered to what degree the skills learned in these simulations were actually applied back on the job. Going one step further, College Pro decided to replace the simulated situations with on-the-job learning facilitated through the existing management structure rather than dedicated "outside" trainers. Searching for a model to represent this new approach, College Pro looked at the methods used to train and certify ski instructors. Typically, ski instructors are certified through a staged process, with a certified examiner observing the ski instructor in action. When someone reaches the highest level, he or she is able to serve as an examiner, certifying others to be ski instructors. This approach served as the prototype for the "College Pro College."

Today, through the "College Pro College," almost all learning is completed in a combination of learning "on-line" and classroom learning and is fully integrated into the completion of daily job responsibilities. The most important characteristic of the learning process is that it is the responsibility of and led by the line management of the company, from CEO to presidents, to vice presidents to general managers, and then to franchise managers. For example, each general manager has a list of competencies that he or she is working on developing. After studying and receiving coaching, the general manager then contacts an "examiner," a manager who has mastered these skills. The examiner then observes the person demonstrating the skill in a real-life situation, *giving the general manager a rating based on how well the skill was exhibited. Afterwards, the examiner provides coaching and helps the manager to set new learning objectives. It is typical for College Pro's senior executives to serve as examiners during their travels in the field.*

At major company meetings, people who have been certified in a leadership skill competency receive a diploma. But the diploma is different from a normal college diploma. While it is meant to be displayed on a wall, it is designed so it can be opened up and new skills written into it as they are mastered. In this way, the diploma becomes a symbol of both College Pro's and the employees' commitment to continuous learning.

In addition, College Pro has tried to take the idea of integrating work and learning a step further. The annual meeting is now designated as an organizational learning event during which each business unit makes a presentation that includes:

- *What did you plan to do last year?*
- *What were the actual results, and why?*
- *What learnings do you take away from your experiences last year?*
- *Based on your learnings, what are the strategic themes for the upcoming years?*

These learnings are then summarized for the company as a whole and strategic learning themes are established for the upcoming year.[1]

College Pro is an example of an entrepreneurial organization that has built success not just on its product or service but also on continuous learning. Over the years, Paul Woolner of Woolner, Lowy & Associates, Toronto, has worked closely with a variety of start-up, entrepreneurial companies such as College Pro.[2] Observing these firms from their beginning, through periods of rapid growth, to phases of relative maturity, he has had a unique opportunity to watch the evolution of their learning processes. In fact, he has observed that these firms often pass through a definable set of stages on their way to becoming learning organizations, in which work and learning have become one. These stages are captured in a five-stage developmental model of the learning organization (Figure 8.1).

Figure 8.1. The Five Stages of the Learning Organization: Integrating Work and Learning.

Stage Five	INTEGRATING WORK AND LEARNING	PRECIPITATOR OF A NEW STAGE
Stage Four	IDENTIFYING AN ORGANIZATION LEARNING AGENDA	systemic skills and work integrity
Stage Three	BRINGING LEARNING INSIDE THE ORGANIZATION	strategic linkage
Stage Two	TREATING LEARNING AS A CONSUMABLE	economies of scale
Stage One	WORKING WITH NO INTENTIONAL LEARNING PROGRAMS	first awareness of need

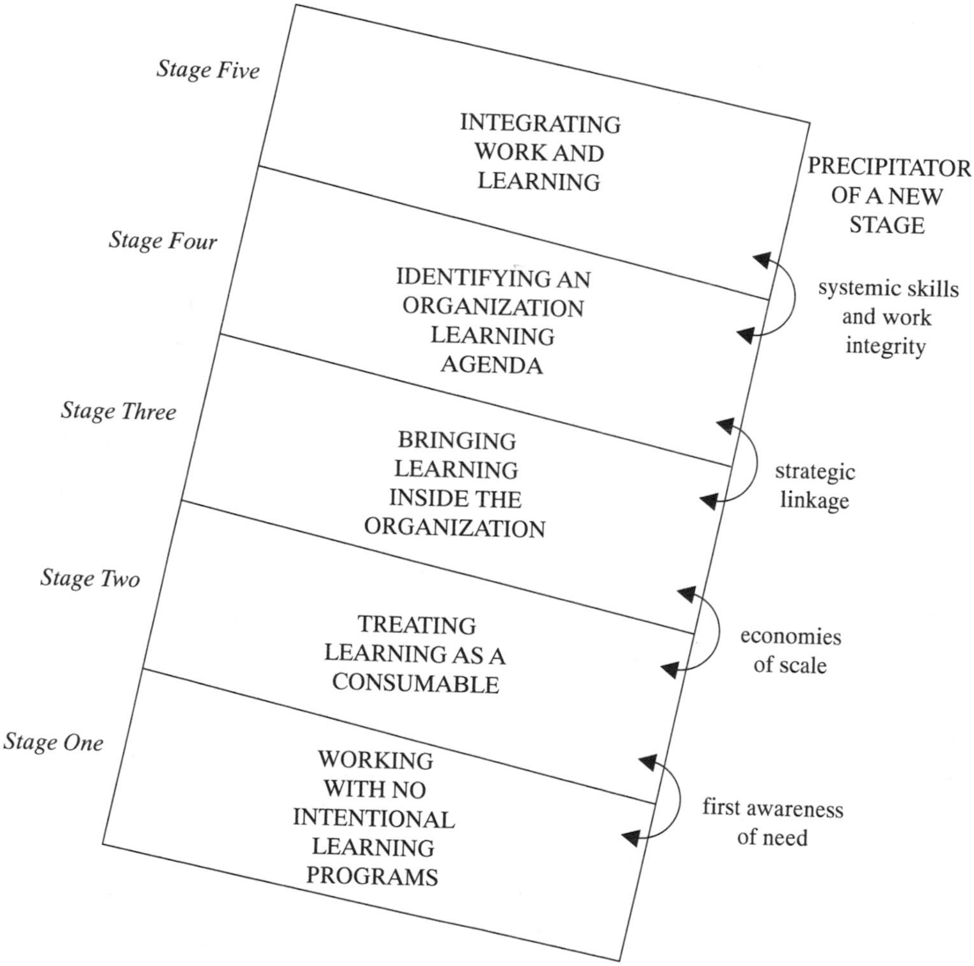

Source: Woolner and Lowy, 1993. Used by permisssion.

In the first stage, which corresponds to the early life of an organization, a great deal of learning and adaptation is taking place. However, this learning often goes unnoticed, since it occurs unintentionally as firms figure out how to carve out market niches, successfully contend with established rivals, and effectively produce products and deliver services. In the second stage, an attempt is made to increase and institutionalize learning through formal training and educational programs. Programs are most often undertaken outside of the organization. Training is viewed as a consumable product to be awarded as a gift during good times. It may also be seen as a "magic bullet" that will fix whatever performance problems individuals in the firm might be having. In the third stage, an attempt is made to ensure that training has a measurable impact on job performance. At this phase, more training is provided within the organization in order to ensure application to job responsibilities and to achieve economies of scale as the participant base grows. Programs still tend to be somewhat arbitrarily chosen and are often seen as "flavor of the year" initiatives. In the fourth stage, an important shift occurs: learning needs are established based upon the strategic business issues facing the organization. The organization itself is seen as needing to develop skills and knowledge, and it is the organization's learning agenda that serves to drive an ambitious, targeted series of training and educational programs. However, in Stage Four, most learning still occurs through off-the-job, classroom-based programs.

At the fifth stage, an important transformation occurs. Woolner explains:

> An organization moves to Stage Five when the realization and commitment has grown among its leadership that it must move learning, as much as possible, out of the classroom and into day-to-day work for learning to bring maximum benefit to the organization. Stage Five involves the alignment of all organization systems toward the achievement of performance through learning. It is a whole systems approach to an understanding of improving organizational perfor-

mance through learning. Similar to Stage One, learning is integrated into people's day-to-day work. At Stage Five, however, it is explicit and planned compared to the informality of Stage One [1992, p. 8].

At the fifth stage, as in the first, learning is a natural process, emerging from the intimate interchange between people and the central tasks required to get the job done. But unlike the first stage, learning does not just happen; it is encouraged, supported, accelerated, and rewarded through the development of formal learning systems.

Must companies go through all five stages to become learning organizations? Not necessarily. According to Woolner, it is not only possible but also increasingly necessary to design firms from their inception with the explicit purpose of becoming Stage Five learning organizations.

This chapter will describe the types of learning systems that organizations develop as they move toward a full integration of work and learning. These integrated learning systems must be constructed at three different organizational levels:

- The individual level
- The team level
- The organizational level

The three levels of learning are not and should not be seen as distinct and mutually exclusive. They work together, with individual learning serving as the spark for the learning of groups, and team learning igniting the collective learning of the entire organization. And the interaction works in both directions. Organizational learning often leads to team learning, which frequently drives individual learning.

Enhancing Individual Learning

Think about the learning that occurs in your organization. Do pictures similar to these flash before your mind's eye?

- A senior executive is attending a three-day executive seminar put on by a leading consulting firm or a major business school. At the front of the room, the seminar leader is pointing to a chart displayed prominently on a screen, explaining the intricacies of a particular new insight, model, or discovery. Sitting pensively, listening intently, the executive then begins to probe the potential practicality of its application back on the job.
- A middle manager is in a U-shaped seminar room, participating in a corporate training program aimed to increase the manager's sensitivity to and skill at handling the specific people issues he or she faces each day on the job.
- A frontline worker is in a high-tech training room, sitting attentively in front of the latest technical equipment, mastering the newest innovation with the tutoring of a technical expert.

What do these images have in common? Each occurs away from the work situation. To borrow a computer term, learning is taking place *off-line*—not on the job. The value to individuals of off-line learning through formal training and educational programs should not be discounted. However, there is a great deal of on-line learning that occurs each day with every member of every organization. People acquire new knowledge as they deal with customers and suppliers. They gather expertise as they repeat and hone their capabilities in the trial-and-error process of making plans happen. And they create new knowledge and expertise as they confront problems and situations never seen before. Learning organizations recognize the pervasiveness and potential potency of such on-line learning and develop systems to encourage it.

When asked to envision individual learning in their companies, members of learning organizations might come up with some images like the following:

- For six months, an engineer is assigned to a task force to investigate the feasibility of a new product introduction. Also on the task force is a marketing manager and a financial analyst. After returning to his original job responsibilities six months later, the engineer now appreciates the need to analyze market needs and financial implications at the early stages of research on a new product design.

- A new machinery operator, although finished with training, has lunch with an experienced co-worker, who explains the insights she gained over the past several year regarding ways to get equipment fixed fast and minimize downtime.

- In a highly seasonal business, every employee is required each year to become cross-trained in another job to be able to assist during periods of peak work load. As a result, individuals find they possess a broad sense of the organization that enhances their ability to fix problems, identify resources, and maintain working relationships.

All of these—and an infinite list of other such examples—are recognized by learning organizations as valid and appropriate ways for individuals to develop new skills and knowledge. But rather than just hoping that on-line learning happens, learning organizations actively encourage, promote, and support such learning.

Mark Cheren of Strategic Learning Services describes three areas in which learning organizations take action to foster continuous on-line learning:

> *Communication.* Learning organizations explain to all
> employees the importance of continuous, on-the-job
> learning and that such learning is a responsibility shared
> by the individual and the organization. As part of this
> step, it is important to identify and communicate a learn-
> ing agenda for the organization. The agenda identifies
> those critical areas that members believe are the most im-
> portant for the organization to develop new skills and
> knowledge in, such as obtaining a better understanding of
> the firm's markets, developing methods for reducing the
> cycle time of new product introductions, and improving
> customer satisfaction.
>
> *Support.* Learning organizations take steps to support each
> person's learning initiatives. While most companies only

keep records of or provide reimbursement for formal training, Cheren suggests that on-line learning be equally le-
gitimized through records and funding. Moreover, he
recommends that performance management systems be
modified to recognize and reward individual learning. In
addition, he advocates that supervisors be trained to become learning consultants, helping individuals to identify
learning needs, assisting in the development of approaches to acquiring the skills and knowledge, and over-
coming roadblocks and problems.

Resources. Learning organizations provide a full range of
resources for learning. So that this can happen, training
and human resource professionals need to modify their
traditional roles as designers of company-managed training programs to become facilitators of individual and
team-managed learning activities. Skill inventories should
be developed to identify who in the organization possesses
what expertise, and then this information should be made
readily available to people as support for their own learning. And resource centers should be established where people can go to receive information and help with their
learning.[3]

Enhancing Team Learning

Team learning provides the bridge between personal learning and
organizational learning (Figure 8.2). It is through team learning
that the personal knowledge and perceptions of individual members
can be transformed into the collective learning of a group and then
made available to the organization at large. As a result, learning
organizations engage in ambitious efforts to develop their capacities
for team learning.

One key to strengthening team learning is to promote the
open exploration and confrontation of differences among members
of the organization. Openly acknowledging differences is often not
as easy as it may sound. Individuals in organizations develop elaborate methods of self-protection, which Argyris (1989) refers to as
defensive routines: "An organizational defensive routine is any pol-

Figure 8.2. Learning Systems Bridge.

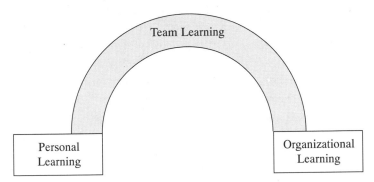

icy, practice, or action that prevents the people involved from being embarrassed or threatened, and at the same time, prevents them from learning how to reduce the causes of the embarrassment or threat" (p. 7). Defensive routines account for reasons why long-standing, obvious errors in organizations are often left uncorrected. Risks are avoided. Original premises are left unquestioned. Disconfirming data are withheld.

To Argyris, defensive routines are particularly insidious because they tend to be self-sealing. That is, not only do defensive routines tend to obscure important organizational realities, they also serve to cover up the cover-up, camouflaging the defensive routine itself. Here is a four-step recipe for creating a self-sealing defensive routine (1989, p. 9):

1. Bypass embarrassment and threat whenever possible.
2. Act as though you are not bypassing them.
3. Don't discuss steps one and two while they are happening.
4. Don't discuss the undiscussability of the undiscussable.

Uncovering Defensive Routines

Chris Argyris and colleagues over the years have conducted numerous workshops with senior management groups to help them

uncover and deal with defensive routines during strategy plan-
ning and implementation sessions (Argyris, 1989). Sessions typi-
cally begin with senior management teams identifying strategic
issues or problems they want to address. After receiving training
to create awareness of and skill in uncovering defensive routines,
teams begin formulating their plans and designing their imple-
mentation strategies. During the sessions, consultants help the
team to become aware of the defensive routines and to "discuss
the undiscussable."

For instance, in one organization, managers revealed a de-
fensive routine of complying with senior executive decisions even
if they believed that the decisions were wrong. Through this pro-
cess, individuals became "aware of the inconsistencies and gaps
that one produced through one's behavior. . . . Each participant
also learned why the others did not discuss his or her inconsisten-
cies and gaps. . . . Their doing so produced conditions in which
important technical and business information tended to be inac-
cessible, ambiguous, and/or vague" (Argyris, 1989, p. 13). Argyris
worked with the team to establish new norms that allowed the
group to openly confront differences, even if the differences were
with top management. Plans were then made for the group to
integrate these norms over a period of several months.

Recognizing the pervasiveness of defensive routines, learning
organizations employ a variety of methods to establish norms that
value honest, direct confrontation of problems, limitations, and
failures. They use 360 degree feedback, in which managers receive
feedback from everyone around them, including peer managers,
subordinates, superiors, even customers and suppliers. In addition,
conventional methods such as employee attitude surveys can pow-
erfully serve to establish norms of discussion in which no topic
must be avoided. And upward appraisal methods, in which performance discussions include subordinates' input and evaluation, are
powerful approaches for sending this message of openness to
feedback.

The Management Challenge at Royal Dutch/Shell

Royal Dutch/Shell has established and formalized an innovative way to encourage team learning through what they call the management challenge. Here is how it works.

Each year, executives from one division, often a unit located in a different part of the world, spend a week at another division interviewing people, reviewing records, and observing the operation. They seek to ask the questions that might not otherwise get asked and to uncover blind spots that might normally be ignored. At the end of the week, the visiting manager issues a challenge to the host executive. This challenge is meant to represent the most important business issue that needs to be addressed by the host division. The challenge is openly posted at the division and also reported back to corporate headquarters. The visiting managers are evaluated based upon the quality of the challenge. And the host managers are held accountable for addressing the challenge over the next year.[4]

Minority Reports at Motorola

According to the Wall Street Journal, *Motorola's amazing ability to act both with the nimbleness of a small entrepreneurial company and with the resources and assurance of the powerful, complex international company that it is, is rooted in its creation of a "cult of conflict."*

Motorola employs a variety of means to promote open, often uncomfortable, and frequently embarrassing confrontation and dissent that few other firms would tolerate. The example for this action is set at the highest senior levels. For instance, the Wall Street Journal *reported that two of Motorola's most esteemed executives have been known to taunt and confront each other, often with a few obscenities thrown in, in front of the board of directors.*

But the ability to disagree, even with your superiors, is not just a perquisite of executives; it is a right and obligation of every employee. This expectation is embodied by a process called the minority report, in which every person is able to submit a report to his or her boss's boss if it is felt that ideas are not being listened to or supported. And it is generally considered bad form for any reprisal to occur as a result of an employee filing a minority report. In fact, a minority report is credited for initiating the corporation's most ambitious project ever, a satellite named Iridium that is scheduled by 1997 to link cellular phone communications around the entire world.[5]

Action Learning

An especially powerful means of improving the team learning capacity of organizations is *action learning*. Action learning is an approach to management training and development first implemented in England in the 1940s, and today it is experiencing fairly widespread application in the United States (Marsick, Cederholm, Turner, and Pearson, 1992).

Before describing the technique of action learning, let us look at its underlying philosophy. The origination of action learning is generally credited to Reg Revans. An athlete and Cambridge physicist, Revans was intrigued by the relationship between action and learning. At its simplest level, action learning is learning by doing. However, Revans is quick to point out that action learning, unlike learning by doing, does not try to emulate what has been done before; instead, it probes the unknown by posing previously unasked questions. In much the same way, he distinguishes action learning from traditional education and training (1991, p. 8): "Most education, and practically all training, is concerned in passing on the secrets and the theories of yesterday. . . . But if today is significantly different from yesterday, and tomorrow is likely to be very different from today, how shall we know what to teach?"

There are three major characteristics of action learning. First, it focuses on real problems, problems that are of current importance and significance to the organization. The best problems are those that cannot be solved through rigorous analysis but those that require intuition and judgment. Second, it focuses on social interaction. Small groups provide the resources for learning. Members come together at regular meetings to discuss their problems and propose solutions, sharing and clarifying assumptions and expectations. Third, action learning is aided by an external resource person who facilitates the process and aids the group through the development stages by helping them to ask the right questions.

What does action learning look like? First, a small group of individuals are brought together. These can be people doing the same job. This so-called learning set starts by identifying the real-world problems they want to learn how to deal with. They receive some background training on the concept of action learning. And in many cases, they might receive some programmed instruction about what is already known about the topic or area of interest, although this training component is generally kept fairly informal and limited. The teams are then led by a facilitator to ask "discriminating questions"—tough questions that get at underlying issues and assumptions about the problems being studied. The group also asks three questions to pinpoint where they can go for support and help:

1. Who knows? (Who can we find to help understand all this?)
2. Who cares? (Who is committed to solving this?)
3. Who can? (Who has the power to take action to address the problem?)

Then, over the course of several months (five or six is normal), the sets go through a process of taking action and coming back to reflect, ask questions, develop new actions, and test them out. A basic concept of action learning is that one really does not know what one knows until it is put into action.

Action Learning at Prudential Assurance

Action learning for district field managers of the U.K. division of the Prudential Assurance Corporation started in 1983 and has ex-

panded to include additional managerial levels. The basic princi-
ples followed by the designers of the program were that the learn-
ing vehicle would be a current real-life problem "owned" by the
individual. The learning groups, consisting of six managers mixed
with respect to age, experience, ability, and geographic location,
learned with and from each other as they discussed their prob-
lems and planned their actions.

Through monthly interactions with their team members
they built plans that they tested in the field. Outside training was
only offered when a specific need was identified that could not
be met using the group's existing skills or knowledge. Members
were given ample opportunity to reflect on the effectiveness of
their actions before taking the next step.

The degree of success obtained by individual participants
in the different learning groups was found to be related to several
factors. Managers who were willing to tackle broad-based prob-
lems and systematically work on the problem between group
meetings tended to be more successful action learners. Managers
who questioned assumptions and norms and willingly gave and
received criticism also were more successful action learners. A
final key factor that characterized managers who were successful
in the program was their ability to listen to other people's ideas
and then put them into practice on their problems.[6]

Action Learning at General Electric

James Noel (1992), manager of executive education at General
Electric, and Ram Charan, previously of Harvard Business School,
describe an action learning approach to enhancing the global
thinking of GE executives.

The program started in Heidelberg, Germany, with the first
week consisting of the formation of teams and the use of peer and
subordinate feedback to assess participant needs for professional
development. Executives were also introduced to key European
business leaders, opinion makers, and government officials and

received lectures regarding the subtleties of working in a multi-cultural business environment.

During the second week, the emphasis shifted to group projects. Each team traveled across Europe, interviewing from sixty to seventy customers, suppliers, analysts, and GE representatives, while at the same time becoming familiar with local culture, language, currency, legislation, and tax laws, as well as consumer preferences for national brands.

During the last two days in Europe, the team assembled a final report. Immediately upon returning to the United States, teams made presentations of the report to various business units, discussing the potential actions that could be taken with each division. The final course activity was a session with CEO Jack Welch in which projects were discussed and issues were raised that related to leadership and values in GE's emerging global corporate environment.[7]

Enhancing Organizational Learning

We have discussed individual learning and team learning. Let us now turn to the collective learning of the organization as a whole, which integrates both the learning of individuals and groups.

Measuring Organizational Learning

There is an old maxim about quality that says, to improve anything, it must be measured. There are attempts under way to provide organizations with means of assessing the extent to which they are learning organizations. One of the first was Udai Pareek's Organizational Learning Diagnostics (OLD) survey. Pareek (1988, pp. 131–132) suggests the following assessment and development steps for learning organizations:

1. Experts and experienced creative practitioners are invited to share their ideas with members of the organization.
2. Employees are encouraged to attend external programs.

3.   Experiences and concerns of the organization are shared with other organizations.
4.   Employees are encouraged to experiment.
5.   Innovations are rewarded.
6.   Periodic meetings are held for sharing results of experiments.
7.   Periodic meetings are held for sharing ongoing experiments.
8.   Employee seminars on new developments are organized.
9.   Task groups are created for implementing and monitoring new projects and experiments.
10. Detailed plans reflecting contingency approaches are prepared.
11. Task groups are created to examine common elements between old practices and innovations.
12. Newly proposed practices are linked with known practices.
13. Records of experiences are maintained.
14. Periodic meetings chaired by top or senior management are held to review innovations.
15. Relevant existing skills are utilized in implementing change.
16. Task groups are created for data-based critiquing of the innovations.
17. Periodic meetings are held to review and share experiences.
18. Task groups are created to evaluate and report on plus-and-minus aspects of innovations.
19. Task groups are created to follow up on experiments.
20. Widespread debates are held on experiences of implementation.
21. Realistic appraisals are made of the support needed for continued use of innovations.
22. Implementation plans are modified when experience indicates that modification is needed.
23. Various groups are encouraged to prepare alternative forms of implementation.[8]

Pareek's OLD has proven an effective way for firms to assess their organizational learning abilities and to develop plans for continuous improvement.

The American Society for Training and Development's Learning Organization Network also set out to create a system for measuring the degree to which any given firm is a learning organization.[9] A pilot study was conducted with seventeen firms engaged in learning efforts. The study began by asking interviewees to identify a specific organizational change initiative. A series of questions were then asked to determine:

- Whether the change effort was a single strategy or an integrated effort
- Whether the impact was localized or systemic
- Whether the learning was single or double loop
- Whether competences were being developed primarily in individuals or additionally in teams or larger systems

It was the view of the researchers that to be considered a learning organization a firm must have change initiatives that meet four criteria: (1) they must be integrated change efforts, (2) they must be systemic change efforts, (3) they must exhibit double-loop learning, and (4) they must include team and organization learning. Only five of the seventeen firms interviewed met all four criteria. As a result, according to the investigators, only those companies could be considered learning organizations.

In addition, Michael O'Brien (1993) has developed a comprehensive one-hundred-item survey called "The Learning Organization Profile." The written survey instrument is divided into ten categories:

1. Strategy/Vision
2. Executive Practices
3. Managerial Practices
4. Organization/Job Structure
5. Performance Goals/Feedback
6. Training and Education
7. Information
8. Interpersonal
9. Rewards/Recognition
10. Individual and Team Development

In each category, a series of detailed questionnaire items determines to what degree the organization "has woven a continuous and enhanced capacity to learn, adapt and change into the very fabric of its character" (p. 2). Respondents are asked to rate to what degree their organizations reflect such traits of learning organizations as follow:

- Learning and innovations flow up as well as down the hierarchy.
- Educational programs include information and skill training on learning how to learn from one's own experience and from others.
- We share our expertise through informal conversations and "story telling," learning from each other.
- Executives speak about the connections between continuous learning, continuous improvement, quality, and business results. [10]

Improving Organizational Learning

Measuring the degree to which a firm is a learning organization is not enough. It is also essential to help firms to increasingly become learning organizations. We are especially intrigued by the idea of designing collective learning events for entire firms aimed at helping them develop their learning capacities. For example, in Chapter Four we outlined the use of search conferences, first proposed by Fred Emery and Eric Trist of the Tavistock Institute. The unique feature of this approach is the bringing together of representatives from the entire organizational system into a single learning process.

Another approach pioneered by the Tavistock Institute is that used in the Leicester conference (Miller, 1989). Built upon the T-group method of experiential learning developed at the National Training Laboratories in the United States, Britain's Tavistock method was always somewhat different—interested more in exploring the group and organization, rather than the individual, as the primary learning subjects. The Leicester conference is a direct inheritance from Kurt Lewin, who viewed groups or organizations as possessing characteristics and properties that are more than and different from those of their individual members. "To be sure," Eric Miller comments, "it has always been characteristic of the Leicester model that the focus of interpretation has been on the dynamic of the group as a whole, and not as individuals" (p. 6).

A typical conference is fourteen days long, often ten to twelve hours long each day. Each conference is organized around a primary task—a strategic mission that links members and forms a central purpose for the conference. The primary task of a recent Leicester conference was as follows: "To provide opportunities to study the exercise of authority in the context of the interpersonal, inter-group and institutional relations that develop within the conference institution" (Miller, 1989, p. 6).

The conference itself is understood to be a temporary organization, and within it are mirrored the same dynamic processes that occur within actual organizations. Embracing an "open systems" view of organizations, the conference attempts to replicate the boundaries that occur at individual, team, and organizational levels as the entity functions within its broader environmental context. These boundaries include:

- The relationships between the organization and its external environment
- The relationships between a group and other groups and the organization as a whole
- The relationships between individuals' roles in subgroups and the organization as a whole

The conference is designed to provoke and explore learning at individual, team, and organizational levels. During a typical conference, there will be events for the entire organization; some for large teams, comprising up to twelve members; and some for teams that are about half that size. But the individual is always considered the starting point for learning. While there may be some conference learning that every participant takes away, it is ultimately up to the individual to determine what he or she will learn from the experience.

Numerous attempts have been made to apply Tavistock's Leicester method to business, government, and social organizations to help them understand and improve learning at individual, team, and, most importantly, organization-wide levels. The following is an example of the Leicester conference's use in higher education.

The Classroom as a Learning Organization

Recently, we conducted a graduate-level exploratory workshop entitled "The Learning Organization" in which the class itself was designed to become a temporary organization. Our aim was to study the organization's learning processes and apply these learnings to firms with which participants were engaged. The workshop design was heavily indebted to Tavistock's Leicester method. The major difference is that actual change interventions were conducted as part of the program. These interventions served as important sources of learning throughout the program.

The course was organized into five eight-hour sessions spread over a ten-week period. Each working session had three components:

- *Community learning*
- *Team learning*
- *Individual learning*

Community Learning

The purpose of the community sessions was to create a pool of collective knowledge regarding organizational learning theory and practice. Generally, each one-day session would start and end with community learning sessions. These sessions were organized around a series of guiding questions that the group used to identify what it did not currently know or understand about learning organizations. These questions were continually modified throughout the conference. During the community learning sessions, people would share new insights and knowledge that they created through their individual learning and team learning processes. An organizational "memory" was established, consisting of a written summary of lessons learned. Over the course of the conference, members gradually took over responsibility for facilitating the community learning sessions.

Team Learning

At the team level, the group formed a series of action learning teams that planned and implemented change interventions in organizations. They included restructuring a department, forming strategic partnerships with suppliers, and improving the effectiveness of a national conference of a major professional association. At each session, participants would assess their current knowledge, uncover assumptions, and develop an action plan that could be implemented before the next session. At the next session, the team would reflect on what worked and what did not, searching for first-level learnings (symptomatic or single-loop learnings), second-level learnings (systemic or double-loop learning), or third-level learnings (learning-to-learn or deutero-learning).

Individual Learning

Each workshop participant identified an organization that he or she had access to. The student then conducted an assessment of the learning processes of this organization at individual, team, and organization-wide levels using interviews, questionnaires, and reviews of documents. The student then wrote a "consultant's report" that provided specific recommendations regarding how the firm could improve its individual, team, and organizational learning.

At the end of the five-session course, the entire learning community reconvened to identify several collective learnings:

- *A surprising amount of pain and frustration accompanies significant learning.*
- *The anxieties that are provoked by facing unknown situations both impede and propel learning.*
- *The power of open dialogue forces people to face what they do not know, and, paradoxically, to create a safe environment for learning.*
- *Ultimately, learning is a private and personal phenomenon. For example, several students found the lack of structure to be*

*an impediment, while others found any structure to be con-
fining and limiting.*

In this chapter, we examined how learning organizations make learning a way of life at individual, team, and organization-wide levels. In the next chapter, we explore how learning organizations seek to become self-organizing systems that continuously change shape as a result of their learning.

9

Become Self-Organizing: Continuously Change Shape in Response to Continuous Learning

In this chapter, we examine how a firm's structure—its particular configurations of roles, relationships, authority, and communication—is a primary determinant of its capacity to learn. In learning organizations, structures are in a process of ongoing flux and modification based upon their learning. In other words, learning organizations are continuously self-organizing systems.

Reengineering for Survival

For several years, one of the key divisions of a major insurance company was experiencing declining market share and profitability. The company appeared cumbersome and bureaucratic compared to its most successful competitors. There had been several rounds of layoffs, and the survival of the division seemed in question. Faced with the urgent necessity to become a flexible and efficient organization, the division undertook an ambitious effort to "reengineer" itself.

Popularized by Michael Hammer (1990), reengineering consists of a radical overhaul of a firm's systems, processes, and structures, often in a fairly short time period, sometimes as little as three to six months. Too many organizations, Hammer suggests, are just rearranging the deck chairs on the Titanic. They often need a clean start. "Reengineering," Hammer writes, "cannot be planned meticulously and accomplished in small and cautious steps. It's an all-or-nothing proposition with an uncertain result" (1990, p. 105).

The division started the reengineering project by forming a reengineering task force, consisting of representatives from all parts and levels of the organization. The task force then set out to overhaul the company with a six-month target for implementation. The team started by asking several key questions:

- How can we organize ourselves not to complete tasks but to achieve results?
- How can we restructure so decisions are made by the people doing the work where the work is being done?
- How can we merge currently discrete responsibilities into whole tasks where, as much as possible, the internal customer and internal suppliers are the same?
- How can we use information and communication technology to leverage our limited resources throughout the firm?
- How can we take processes that were performed in a linear sequence and integrate them so they can be performed at the same time?

The team made several recommendations. First, it suggested that the company be structured around three business units, each responsible for one of the key central "outcomes" of the company. It recommended flattening the organization, reducing levels of management from eight to three, using information technology and training to provide individuals with the capability to make most insurance decisions on the spot with customers. And it reengineered its major product development process through cross-functional teams that linked market research, product development, product testing, and product introduction into a single integrated process.

Without major exception, the recommendations were accepted and are currently being implemented. However, now *about six months into the implementation plan, the company is, according to most reports, in turmoil. "We're in shock," one middle manager reported. "People are unsure of what their jobs are, and, in many cases, if they will have jobs. Things just aren't working like we thought that they would." In addition, both productivity and customer service indicators have experienced dramatic declines compared to a year earlier.*

Many of these problems were expected; yet, to the organization, they are still gut-wrenching to go through. Today, the organization is struggling with the long-term issue of how it can continue to redesign itself as it goes along, rather than needing to undergo the radical upheaval of a major restructuring. To achieve that goal, it is planning to create permanent reengineering teams that will be responsible for working out the problems of the newly implemented system and modifying the system as needed over time. It is also planning an increased reliance upon temporary teams and special-project assignments targeted to deal with the most important challenges facing the organization.

Over recent years, there has been growing interest in the fundamental restructuring of businesses, exemplified by the question, If we were to start all over, is this how we would do things? As a result, many corporations—some facing crises, others not—are trimming down, losing fat, and increasing versatility through massive restructuring. The benefits, Kanter (1989) suggests, are hard to dispute, since most restructuring "involves not simply reducing and not simply asset-shuffling but something more: an effort to find the form that will permit doing more with less. Spending less but yet creating more value" (p. 58). Restructured corporations tend to be flatter, more decentralized, and less hierarchical.

Massive restructuring also has a dark side. Like any radical surgery, it is risky, and some patients do not come out of the operation alive. It throws firms into turmoil with a confusion of roles, a diffusion of energy, and an upsurge of human emotion that can bring day-to-day operation almost to a standstill. Moreover, restructuring can go too far. Occasionally, cuts aimed at trimming excess fat end up slicing into the very muscle of organizations. And in a fervent desire to break from the shackles of old mind-sets, restructuring is implemented with the premise that anything associated with the preexisting structure is, by definition, devoid of value and should not be retained.

We are not suggesting that major overhauls of organizations are not needed. For many firms, radical surgery may be essential just to stay alive. But, in our view, restructuring is not a management practice that should be replicated in the future. Like an extreme diet-and-exercise regimen prescribed for people who need to lose a great deal of weight rapidly, it may be necessary, but it is not the best approach to keeping in shape. There is no doctor who tells a patient, "Eat all you want and don't exercise for five years, and then I'll put you on a program where you will lose it all in six months." Obviously, this is not healthy for individuals. Nor is it for organizations. For individuals, wellness has to be a way of life. So, too, for organizations.

Instead, learning organizations strive to be continuously self-organizing. Self-organizing systems "are able to learn from their own experience, and to modify their structure and design to reflect what they have learned" (Morgan and Ramirez, 1984, p. 2). For an example of self-organizing systems, look to nature. As Burns and Stalker (1961) have argued, self-organizing systems resemble the "organic" structures of nature (Figure 9.1).

According to Margaret Wheatley, there is probably no more self-organizing a system than a mountain stream:

> This stream has an impressive ability to adapt, to shift the configurations, to let the power balance move, to create new structures. But driving this adaptability, making it all happen, I think, is the water's need to flow. Water answers to gravity, to downhill, to the call of ocean. The forms change, but the mission remains clear. Structures emerge, but only as temporary solutions that facilitate rather than interfere. There is none of the rigid reliance on single forms, on true answers, on past practices that I have learned in business. . . .

Table 9.1. Two Views of the Organization: A Comparison.

Organization as Machine	Organization as Living Organism
The firm's main job is differentiated into precisely defined subtasks, which are executed independently from both other subtasks and the larger purpose of the firm.	Tasks are understood in the context of the total situation and are defined and modified in relation to each other.
Each person has a clearly defined responsibility and role, with procedures and work methods determined by higher levels of the hierarchy.	Individual responsibilities are defined according to the broader purpose of the organization, and not by narrowly prescribed authorities.
It is the purpose of levels in the hierarchy to control individual tasks and to reconcile and coordinate them with the main tasks of the organization.	Coordination, communication, and control occur through a network of lateral, diagonal, and vertical patterns.
Communication is essentially vertical.	Power and authority are awarded according to the knowledge and skills needed for specific issues, and not purely by hierarchical rank.

Organizations lack this kind of faith, faith that they can accomplish their purposes in various ways and that they do best when they focus on direction and vision, letting transient forms emerge and disappear [1992, pp. 15–16].

This mountain stream is in a continuous process of regeneration and self-transformation, maintaining its core identity while continuously changing form, both adapting to and modifying its surroundings at the same time.

In the remainder of this chapter we will outline the principles of self-organizing systems and describe the process through which firms can move to become increasingly self-organizing.

The Principles of Self-Organization

How does an organization become self-organizing? Since the 1940s, London's Tavistock Institute of Human Relations, most notably through the work of Eric Trist and Fred Emery, has pioneered the creation of flexible, adaptive organizational structures.[1] It all started with a visit to the coal mines in Yorkshire, England: "Imagine a factory, damp, dark, and dangerous, in which workers move their machines daily, extract an ever-changing raw material, transport supplies, equipment, and product through two narrow tunnels, and spend much of each day keeping the walls and ceiling from falling in. Add repetitious, stressful jobs—drilling, cutting, hewing, and building roof supports—and a coercive supervisor: *voila,* you have a work force marked by 2 percent absenteeism, high attrition, frequent accidents, and low productivity" (Weisbord, 1987, pp. 150-151).

But in the late 1940s, a technological breakthrough, short-wall mining, allowed for a fundamental transformation of the workplace, changing not just the technology of doing the work, but the social relationships among the workers as well. This metamorphosis of the coal mines was documented in studies that heralded the beginning of *sociotechnical* systems design, serving as the forebear of today's redesign and reengineering efforts (Trist, Higgin, Murray, and Pollock, 1963).

What did this sociotechnical design consist of? Instead of a group of miners being closely supervised by a foreman, the miners now formed an autonomous work team that collectively shared responsibility for the task and getting the jobs done. Instead of each miner having a fixed role, jobs were interchangeable. Instead of tasks being completed in a rigid order, they could be performed in a variety of different sequences. Instead of possessing highly specialized skills, people were cross-skilled. Instead of status distinctions based on what job people did, all members of the team were equal. Instead of external quality inspection and supervision, the team managed itself. Instead of shifts operating individually, with separate production and quality goals, they worked together to achieve joint targets (Weisbord, 1987). The results? Productivity, absenteeism, and accident rates all experienced dramatic improvements.

Over the years, members and associates of the Tavistock Institute have refined and replicated the sociotechnical approach in numerous settings, including manufacturing settings, high technology firms, health care institutions, and government agencies. In many cases, design efforts centered around the organization of the company into business teams that are then managed by autonomous (or semiautonomous) work teams. But to understand sociotechnical redesign merely as the creation of autonomous work teams is reductionistic, turning a rich set of insights about organizations into the application of a single technique. Underlying sociotechnical redesign are the following core design goals:

- Becoming holographic
- Minimizing structure and maximizing autonomy
- Mirroring the variety in the environment
- Continuously changing shape

Become Holographic

In a three-dimensional hologram, every part of the picture carries the image of the whole. If one were to smash a hologram into pieces (such as a 3-D image of Elvis), each fragment would contain a mini-picture of the whole Elvis. It is this same holographic quality, this ability to take any of the organization's pieces and use it to construct the whole, that helps endow learning organizations with their continuous self-organizing capacity. To promote continuous learning and self-organization, each individual should possess, as much as possible, the skills and knowledge needed to complete the entire task the unit is charged with completing.

Earlier in this book, we described several actions that learning organizations take to increase their holographic qualities, such as building a shared, common vision and a heightened awareness of external environments. Simply stated, it should be possible to take any member of the organization and ask him or her to give you some sense of the firm's overriding purpose and some idea of what is going on with competitors, technologies, and markets. If the organization is holographic, every person's answers will be the same.

But to be truly holographic, firms also need to build in the feature of *redundancy*. Simply stated, redundancy means providing people with the capability to perform a wide range of different tasks in an organization. For every job, there should be multiple-skilled backups and replacements who can step in when the work load increases and when problems arise. By building redundancy, firms build slack resources that are capable of being flexibly moved around to fit different needs.

At first glance, redundancy may appear to impede efficiency, increasing fat rather than decreasing it. Certainly, some time and effort must be expended when building redundancy into organizations. But the payback often comes quickly and is surprisingly dramatic, producing high levels of flexibility in adapting to the daily ebb and flow of production requirements, increasing the firm's capacity to move resources to where they are needed during crises, and providing each member of the firm with the ability to have an impact on broad, systemic aspects of the business.

For example, a small manufacturing company is organized around twelve- to fourteen-person teams in which each team member has been certified to perform several other jobs on the team. An existing standard requires that each member be certified in one new skill every six months. In addition, to be eligible to be certified in a new skill, each member must have certified another person in his or her primary job. The organization, over recent years, has developed remarkable flexibility and adaptability. It is evident every day in simple ways. When there is a bottleneck on the line holding up production, team members take the initiative to leave their primary jobs and move to other jobs and fill in. Once an hour, team members huddle at flip chart easels to review current productivity and quality levels, jointly planning how to best deploy resources for the next hour. Moreover, skill redundancy has allowed team members to be freed up from production to serve on a variety of cross-functional teams dealing with new product introductions, supplier management, and engineering issues. This is truly what self-organization looks like.

Minimize Structure and Maximize Autonomy

There is probably no more radical departure from traditional bureaucratic structures than the principle of *minimal critical specification*. This design principle recognizes that organizations require some structure to operate effectively and efficiently—such as having some differentiation of functions, some stipulation of standard operating procedures, some division of responsibilities, and some clarity about roles. Such structure should be kept as minimal as possible. It should be used as a starting point, serving as a basis for continuous modification based upon learning.

The concept of minimal critical specification underlies the notion of creating a shared vision of a desired future, which we described in Chapter Four. It is also embedded in the notion of "core competency" (Prahalad and Hamel, 1990). Rather than defining a firm's strategic competitive advantage as a given product or process, the notion of core competencies identifies those underlying capabilities that transcend any given market, such as Sony's superiority in miniaturization or Canon's excellence in imaging and microprocessor controls. Likening a corporation to a tree, Prahalad and Hamel view core competencies as the "roots of competitiveness" from which grow the firm's business units, from which are produced its final fruits, its products. Core competencies do not have a life cycle of growth-maturity-decline, as do products and technologies. Instead, they have the capacity to become stronger over time. Yet keeping core competencies to a critical few is essential. Even the most diverse corporations find that maintaining a competitive advantage in more than a handful of core competencies is difficult, if not impossible.

Related to the concept of minimal critical specifications is the principle of *equifinality*, which simply means that there are many ways to skin a cat. According to this guideline, people, teams, and business units should be given the maximum autonomy to figure out the best way to achieve desired outcomes. Following this principle, there should be increasing localized control of decision making.

Lean, Local, and Open at Hanover Insurance

The once-struggling Hanover Insurance Company is now consistently rated in the top quartile of U.S. insurance companies. In his book Charting the Corporate Mind *(1990), Charles Hampden-Turner attributes Hanover's recent success to its flexibility derived from three factors: leanness, localism, and openness.*

Leanness is a purposeful strategy to remain as efficient,

customer-centered, and quality-focused in the good times as is demanded during the bad times. From Hanover's perspective, any future need to endure the suffering of restructuring would be the end result of years of mismanagement and fattiness. However, leanness does not mean slashing costs. It means adding value. Somewhat surprisingly, as expense ratios have been cut, expenditures for staff development have increased.

Localism is a commitment to a unique structure that paradoxically embraces the best of both decentralism and centralism. Above all else, it means that major decisions are made at divisional locations and not at headquarters. Doing so allows adaptation to a regionally diverse marketplace. But most importantly, according to Hampden-Turner, it also provides the opportunity for divisions to learn: "A crucial part of Hanover's philosophy [is] that people grow, learn, and fulfill their potentials through making decisions and taking responsibility for the outcome" (1992, p. 23). But the corporate office maintains a strong role as a coach, defining the criteria for assessing performance, evaluating branches based on these criteria, and providing assistance for continually improved performance. Headquarters also attempts to serve as a corporate "brain," integrating knowledge gained in one part of the firm and disseminating it to other parts.

Openness is the establishment of norms that promote the continuous search for better ways. "Effective openness," Hampden-Turner observes, "reconciles advocacy with inquiry, and listens with a genuine willingness to qualify what is advocated in a shared quest for the solutions of greatest merit. . . . You cannot learn to perform better if managers are too squeamish to contrast a mediocre performance with a higher standard" (p. 24). The real payoff of leanness, localism, and openness is to ensure that Hanover learns faster than its chief competitors.[2]

Mirror the Variety in the Environment

The study of natural evolution tells us that, when it comes to the survival of the fittest, those species with a wider variety of adaptive responses will be the ones to survive, allowing them to respond flexibly to new situations. This principle is called the "law of requisite variety" (Ashby, 1952). What is true in nature is true in business. In rapidly changing, often turbulent business conditions, organizations that possess greater requisite variety than their competition will be the most likely to survive. Requisite variety consists of an organization mirroring the variety and complexity contained in its environment, thereby giving the organization the potential to actively adapt to future uncertainties. Gareth Morgan explains, "Whether we are talking about the creation of a corporate planning group, a research department, or a work group in a factory, [requisite variety] argues in favor of a proactive embracing of the environment in all its diversity. Very often managers do the reverse, reducing variety in order to achieve greater internal consensus. For example, corporate planning teams are often built around people who think along the same lines, rather than around a diverse set of stakeholders who can actually represent the complexity of the problems with which the team ultimately has to deal" (1986, p. 101).

Requisite variety is essential in the people that make up an organization. Learning organizations appreciate the inherent value of assembling a diverse and heterogeneous work force that brings a wide range of approaches, perspectives, and talents to bear on any issue. Cultural diversity is part of the equation. If organizations reflect in microcosm the larger community in which they operate (and for most leading organizations, that is the global community), there are many benefits. Doing so may provide a competitive edge in hiring and retaining a qualified work force, improving customer service to a diverse clientele, and increasing sensitivity to the cultural subtleties of the marketplace. But most significantly, cultural diversity may help ensure that culturally biased mind-sets do not limit the range of alternatives a firm considers when wrestling with any given issue.

What is true for cultural diversity is equally true for functional diversity. Traditionally, firms have tended to emphasize one or two functions—such as engineering, marketing, finance, or production—often to the exclusion of others, staffing up in these areas, providing these disciplines with more influence in decision making, and preferring those with select functional backgrounds for promotion into key senior management positions. But such functional-centrism can limit choice and, therefore, inhibit learning. What is needed is a point of view in which the values, background, and experience of any one function are not, a priori, respected more than others. As a result, learning organizations seek to develop those functional areas that are less mature. For example, if a company's financial expertise is a core competence, the firm may seek to build corresponding marketing or engineering capabilities, recognizing that these may be essential to compete in a marketplace that may be much different tomorrow than it is today. They also attempt to make a person's functional background, by itself, irrelevant for influence and authority in an organization.

In *Managing on the Edge,* Richard Pascale (1990) presents a persuasive case for the importance of requisite variety in preparing firms for continuous learning. In comparing companies with continued resiliency, like Honda, with others characterized by stagnancy, such as General Motors, Pascale observed that the most successful firms possessed an unresolved contention between opposite approaches to running the business. Pascale argues that contention can be produced in any of seven major subsystems: strategy, structure, systems, style, staff, shared values, and skills. For each subsystem, Pascale envisions two polar approaches, as follows:

> Strategy: planned versus opportunistic
> Structure: elitist versus pluralistic
> Systems: mandatory versus discretionary
> Style: managerial versus transformational
> Staff: collegiality versus individuality
> Shared values: hard minds versus soft hearts
> Skills: maximize versus "meta-mize"

Take strategy, for instance. On one hand, an organization might adopt a highly planned approach to developing strategy; on the other hand, the firm might have no formal planning and instead take advantage of opportunities as they arise.

Traditionally, companies have looked at these as either-or choices. That is, each firm determines, intentionally or unintentionally, to be either "elitist" or "democratic." But Pascale suggests that learning organizations see these not as either-or choices but as "and-also" opportunities to create variety within the organization. Therefore, they may seek to be both elitist *and also* democratic, not trying to pick one or the other, not compromising one for the other, but doing both at the same time.

Continuously Change Shape

In learning organizations, form always follows function; that is, the firm generates new structural patterns to fit the tasks at hand. And since the demands upon organizations are in continual flux—based on externally driven forces as well as continuous learning internally—the structure of the organization is also in continuous flux. As Mohrman and Cummings describe (1989), organizations need to possess the capacity for continuous self-design, employing "flexible structures that are continually being modified and improved. They view structures as temporary solutions to current problems and seek to adjust structures to fit changes in strategy, tasks, and environment. . . . Because the emphasis is on organizing, learning, and improving . . . [they] encourage employees to question existing structures and to change them if necessary" (p. 11).

Various labels are used to describe organizations that continually change shape, including *adhocracies* (Waterman, 1990) and *virtual corporations* (Davidow and Malone, 1992). Those of us striving to create learning organizations often prefer the term *network organizations* because of the implied analogy between organizational structure and the human cognitive system (Michaels, 1991). Probably no system is more self-organizing than the human brain's neural network. Composed of over ten billion neurons, the neural network allows information to flow in all directions, forming a continually shifting set of neural connections though which knowledge is created and stored for future use. In the same way, an organization can be envisioned as a giant brain, and each person a node in the neural network that constitutes the firm's cognitive system. Charles Savage (1990) of Digital explains the power of the neural network analogy: "If we were to see ourselves not as boxes but as nodes in a network, not as cogs in a gear but as knowledge contributors and decision points, our support of one another would increase dramatically" (p. 150).

In practical terms, how do organizations continually change shape and form?

- Through the widespread use of temporary organizational structures (project teams, task forces, redesign teams, and so on) to accomplish specific tasks. In Chapter Five, we described the use of a variety of ad hoc structures as a primary means of improvising strategic change.
- By promoting peer-to-peer networking that cuts through the divisions and hierarchies of corporations, allowing somebody who wants to know something to talk to somebody who knows it.
- By adopting some form of matrix management in which parallel organizational structures are established, one across functional lines and one across product or market lines.
- By establishing systems for communicating and sharing knowledge across the entire organization (E-mail, search conferences, knowledge exchanges, and so on). As noted earlier, many firms today are experimenting with the use of computer-based "neural networks," which, by simulating the human neural system, allow for the dissemination and integration of complex information throughout a large, geographically dispersed corporation.

Become Self-Organizing

At the core of our discussion in this chapter, there is a paradox. On one hand, we contend that organizations need to transform themselves into continually self-organizing systems not in need of radical surgery and overhaul. Yet, on the other hand, we also suggest that most firms require radical surgery to become self-organizing. So the question becomes, how do we transform firms into self-organizing systems without violating the basic principle of learning organizations—namely, that change must be learned?

The Best-Laid Plans

Almost two years ago, a mid-sized manufacturing division engaged a consulting firm to coordinate a sociotechnical redesign of the business. Awareness sessions were held with all employees to explain the principles of sociotechnical design, the critical importance of the redesign to the future success of the business, and the need for the involvement and support of everybody to make things happen.

To coordinate the restructuring effort, a redesign team was formed consisting of representatives from throughout the organization. The redesign team spent the better part of a year developing a detailed, three-year implementation plan:

First-Year Plan

- *Restructure into business units organized around the five major tasks of the business.*
- *Select business leaders for each business unit.*
- *Eliminate time clocks.*
- *Disband stand-alone maintenance and quality control functions, incorporating them into the five business teams.*
- *Grant cross-functional teams the responsibility for plant safety and maintenance.*
- *Provide all employees with training in team skills and business management skills.*

Second-Year Plan

- *Replace the plant's existing senior management team with a steering committee composed of leaders and representatives of business teams.*
- *Establish cross-functional teams to handle the purchasing, employment, and community relations functions.*
- *Create an employee-to-employee feedback system.*
- *Begin supplier partnership programs.*
- *Revamp the compensation system to a "pay for skill" system in which team members are paid based upon the degree to*

which they have mastered the skills required by the entire team.

Third-Year Plan

- *Disband engineering, production, and inventory control as distinct functions and incorporate them into business teams.*
- *Eliminate the group leader (supervisor) role.*

These recommendations were made to senior management and corporate officials, and, with only minor changes, they were accepted. The redesign team was replaced by an implementation team, which took over the responsibility for putting the plan into action. Meetings were held with all employees to explain the plan. And a celebration was held to signal the start of an important new chapter in the history of the division.

Yet, six months later, a year and a half after the redesign process was initiated, no fundamental changes had yet taken place. There were several reasons why. The general manager was promoted and the new manager, while generally supportive of the redesign, did not back many of the details of the implementation plan. In addition, several major production problems caused attention and resources to be diverted from the redesign process. A production supervisor summed up the dilemma: "We have to worry about making it through the next few months. Who the hell can think about the next three years?"

What's more, considerable resistance occurred from the middle-management ranks, and several key people threatened to leave the division. Supervisors were concerned about their loss of authority. Professional staff (including those in engineering and purchasing) argued that the plan was not workable and would destroy the integrity of their functions. And finally, ambitious financial performance targets caused corporate headquarters to recommend that the division postpone the implementation of the redesign plan until the next fiscal year.

Meanwhile, out on the shop floor, people felt that the design effort was another program that had come and gone. Moreover, several members of the original redesign team voiced that *they would never volunteer for a company-wide committee again, preferring to "come in each day and just do my job."*

From our experience, the above illustration is all too com-mon. Just as corporations have discovered the futility of implement-ing other types of strategic changes through formal plans and fixed programs, not surprisingly they are discovering the same when they try to restructure companies overnight.

We believe that restructuring must be tempered with respect for the past and an appreciation for the wisdom that often underlies existing organizational systems. Companies are often the way they are for good reason. To some degree, they gradually assumed their cur-rent shapes as evolutionary adaptations to their environments. Unless the business environment is 100 percent different today than it was yesterday (and, in even the most extreme instances, this is unlikely), there needs to be a sorting out of what is valuable from the past from what needs to be eliminated. In fact, there may be important aspects of the organization that need not to be salvaged but to be honed and polished into tomorrow's competitive superiority.

Restructuring also needs to be done with humility. Under ideal circumstances, restructuring should derive from thoughtful, rational analyses of organizations based upon sound, proven prin-ciples. However, this seldom happens. Restructuring is rarely a purely rational process. First, there is a limit to how far rational analysis will take us. Our rationality is, as Herbert Simon (1969) suggests, always "bounded." Organizations are too complex for any person or team to fully understand all of the variables and their interrelationships. Second, there are few universal principles that apply to all organizations in all situations. Finally, restructuring is also a political process, fundamentally altering the power arrange-ments in the firm. It is likely that any decisions will be influenced by these considerations as well.

But most importantly, we believe that restructuring needs to occur through the same strategic learning cycle described in the first few chapters of the book (Figure 9.1).

As described in Chapter Two, the effectiveness of learning

Figure 9.1. Restructuring Cycle.

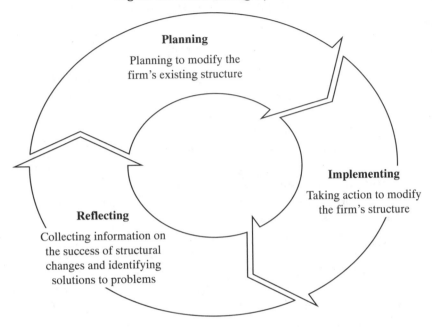

Source: Adapted from Mohrman and Cummings, 1989, p. 116.

can be gauged by the speed, depth, and breadth of learning in each iteration.

What does restructuring look like when it occurs as a journey of strategic learning? For an answer, let us return to the illustration just provided in which the "best-laid plans" of redesigning a manufacturing firm never got off the ground. What could the company do today to employ a learning-based approach to its restructuring? Here are some ideas:

- Replace the detailed implementation road map with a clear, shared vision of the final destination—the end result of a successful sociotechnical redesign.
- Find ongoing opportunities to communicate, support, and nurture this vision, recognizing that the vision will change shape and form over time.

- Learn from the past. Identify those locations in the plant where movement in the desired direction had already begun to take place. Most organizations will be surprised to find out how much there is in the current structure to build upon.
- Develop short-term, targeted implementation plans focused on immediate issues.
- Piggyback on any changes that are happening, such as a new product introduction, a change in technology, or a change in key personnel. Use these as opportunities to introduce key elements of the redesign.
- Allow different business units to find their own ways to the same destination.
- Encourage grass-roots experimentation and innovation.
- Schedule frequent opportunities to reflect on implementation plans, encouraging open dialogue and exploration of progress and difficulties.
- When reflecting upon the cause of implementation roadblocks, carefully examine the underlying assumptions, searching for systemic, double-loop solutions to the problems.
- Continuously summarize the lessons learned and apply them from one situation to the next.

The Best-Laid Plans: Part 2

What happened to the manufacturing firm described in "The Best-Laid Plans" case presented earlier in this chapter? What happened to the company that spent hundreds of hours developing a highly detailed three-year redesign plan and yet, eighteen months later, had not begun to implement the plan?

With the guidance of its new general manager, the division abandoned its detailed road map for redesigning the plant. Yet, at the same time, it reaffirmed its original vision that a new and radically different type of factory would be needed to compete in the next century. At a series of meetings with employees, the general manager acknowledged that he did not know what this plant of the future would look like. Instead, he stressed the need for the plant to start moving in that direction and to discover answers as it went.

A few weeks later, the general manager met with his senior staff at a one-day off-site planning meeting. "Overall, we know what we need to do to keep this division competitive," he observed in his opening comments. "A lot of major change is needed. Yet, I am also sure there are many good things going on in this plant that we can build on. I'd like you to educate me today about what they are." Somewhat tentatively, a few managers began to describe some recent innovations:

- All employees on one production line had become fully cross-trained.
- Another production line had taken responsibility for doing a weekly production schedule.
- Second shift had taken over much of its maintenance and quality control functions (out of necessity because these departments ran with skeletal crews on second shift).

Over thirty specific grassroots changes were soon identified. Everybody was surprised to see how much change had already begun to take place. A plan was then developed to highlight these grassroots initiatives in newsletters and department meetings. In this process, the people who championed these changes were quietly recognized for their accomplishments.

A few months later, the division received news that it had been selected as the production site for a promising new product. An entirely new production line would need to be installed, requiring both new equipment and new staff. While initially small—only about twenty people to start—the prodution line had the potential to swell to over two hundred people within two years.

In initial discussions about the new line, the chief engineer threw out a challenge. "We've talked a lot about teams and the new factory we want to create. Let's stop talking. Let's do something. Let's give it a try and see if it works." After some debate, the decision was made to use this new production line as an experiment in redesign.

The second shift supervisor was selected to serve as team

leader, given that she had been used to running her shift independently and had developed a strong team in the process. After interviewing interested people from throughout the plant, the team leader selected twenty individuals based on their past performance and their team skills.

About three months before production was to begin, the new staff was in place. The team worked closely with engineering to lay out the production line, with purchasing to develop raw material specifications, and with quality control to nail down inspection methods. With the training staff, the team started a series of weekly training programs focused on acquiring the skills needed to self-manage the line.

Today—a year after the "best-laid plan" was abandoned— the rough contours of the redesigned plant are gradually taking shape. For many employees, their daily lives seem unchanged. However, more and more grassroots experiments are emerging, and some have become general practice throughout the plant. At every opportunity, the general manager continues to talk about "a new plant for the next century." In fact, people from throughout the division are using the term next-century plant as shorthand for the evolving vision. And the new team, now with over fifty members, was asked to review its experience and assemble some "lessons learned," which representatives from the team presented to corporate staff at a quarterly update meeting. Finally, and most important, the division has learned a great deal about what it takes to transform itself into "a new plant for the next century."

As appropriate, we have come full circle, returning to the point we made at the beginning of the book: a learning organization approaches strategic change as a journey of learning. In the next section, the Epilogue, we use jazz improvisation as an analogy to summarize and integrate the major themes we have presented.

⨲ Epilogue

Improvising the Future: Learning Organizations and Jazz

Several themes are woven throughout this book: (1) business environments are inherently unpredictable, (2) fixed programs and plans for change seldom produce intended results, and (3) an organization's speed of learning may be its only sustainable competitive advantage.[1] In fact, for an organization to survive it must learn both faster than the change in its business environments and faster than the learning of its chief rivals. Here it is in an equation:

$$\frac{\text{probability}}{\text{of survival}} = \frac{\text{an organization's learning}}{\text{environmental change} + \text{competitor learning}}$$

That is, the chance of any firm surviving is equal to the rate of learning in that organization divided by the sum of the rate of change in its environment and the rate of learning by competitors.

Over the course of the book, we have offered a series of concrete, practical steps that you can take to enhance your organization's inherent capacity to learn how to change faster than both your environment and your competition. But what does it actually feel like to be a member of a learning organization? To answer this question, we turn to jazz music. Analogies can shed light on even the darkest corners of new rooms of thought. We are both fans of jazz music. To us, jazz offers a rich, complex analogy that helps us

176

define for ourselves and explain to others what we mean by learning organizations and what it feels like to be members of learning organizations.[2]

The Freedom to Improvise

The core of jazz is improvisation. Jazz musicians possess both the freedom and the responsibility to improvise, integrating divergent musical forces, continuously transforming them into something unique, and perpetually making each moment new. Improvisation may consist of an exploration of the underlying chord structure or rhythmic pattern of the original composition. It may include an investigation into the historical foundation upon which the composition was based. Or it may simply constitute a spontaneous, creative statement by the performer, expressing his or her own personal musical voice.

No one improvised better than Charlie "Bird" Parker. Bird improvised at lightning speed, often extemporizing unique, one-time-only compositions at four times the pace of other musicians. According to legend, one night Bird was in the midst of an especially complex, high-speed improvisation, the themes of which he had been weaving together and building up for several minutes, when a particularly attractive woman entered the club. In a split second, Bird integrated the tune from "A Pretty Girl Is Like a Melody" into his musical train of thought.

Similarly, members of learning organizations, rather than merely implementing company plans by rote, possess the freedom and responsibility to improvise strategic change. According to Lee Tom Perry (1991), traditional strategic planning is similar to conventional "classical" music, while the improvisational approach to strategy implementation has more in common with jazz: "Traditional strategic plans are like traditional musical format. All of the options are specified by strategic planners, leaving little to the imagination of the managers who have to implement strategy. An improvisational approach to strategy is more like jazz format. It is an open and evolving strategy, allowing for improvisation. Managers formulate and implement strategy together in real-time. The ideal is realized when different managers improvise successful strategies around a common strategic intent. . . . The emphasis is on action and continuous experimentation, not obsessive planning" (p. 51).

In jazz, every performer is to some degree a composer—expected and encouraged to deviate, experiment, and explore the original musical structure. In learning organizations, every employee is to some extent a strategic planner—required and stimulated to improvise upon the central strategy and to act in independent and creative ways to make strategic change happen.

A Collective Sense of Purpose

Here is a surprise to many. The spontaneity of jazz is, in part, an illusion. Great jazz is orchestrated, inspired by a clear sense of intent and direction. In most cases, the structure derives from an underlying harmonic framework, a progression of chords that repeat in a logical pattern. Paradoxically, only by having a limiting structure can musicians improvise. Over the years, jazz musicians have attempted to improvise without such a framework. And it just doesn't work. According to one jazz critic, "When the performer is not bound by stylistic limitations, his improvisations become sketchy and sporadic, he shows flashes of creativity, he plays an interesting measure or two here and there, but his creation suffers in its total impact. Music, improvised or written, if it is to be art, must have direction and purpose" (Ostranski, 1973, p. 74).

Compared to the written, detailed notation relied upon by classical music performers, jazz does not precisely prescribe what musicians are to play. The structure is below the surface, an underlying girder that supports and informs the performance, providing the basis for collective improvisation. While jazz is freer and looser in form than is classical music, individuals must come to each performance with a deeper and clearer understanding of artistic intention. For instance, non-jazz musicians can often sight-read their parts on the spot, following precisely written scores. In jazz, however, the composition is not necessarily on paper; it is internalized by each performer in what is commonly referred to as a head arrangement, a musical composition that exists in the minds of the players.

Similarly, learning organizations seek to establish a clear strategic direction that is loose enough to allow for freedom of expression and creativity in execution. They have a vision that is constantly emerging and developing. A vision that embodies the essence of what the organization must become to survive in the future. A vision that, when compared against today's realities, necessitates continuing quests for better ways. A vision that demonstrates that the organization is not a helpless victim of uncontrollable forces but an active agent that has some power over its own destiny. A vision that is kept purposely broad and open to allow for both the alteration of course over time and the involvement of the organization in the creation of the vision. Half seriously, someone once commented that all you need to do to create a great strategic plan is to tear out every other page.

Dissonance and Syncopation

During a performance, jazz ensembles purposely establish and maintain a sense of disequilibrium that serves as a spark for innovation and creativity. Harmonically, disequilibrium is created through dissonance. In much traditional music, there are rather stringent prescriptions about what sounds should be played at the same time, sounds that blend harmoniously together. In jazz, discordant, cacophonous sounds—sounds that, according to all convention, should not go together—are played as a means of creating a dynamic tension that spurs improvisation. Rhythmically, disequilibrium is generated through syncopation. Syncopation is the act of doing the unexpected, coming down on the offbeat, establishing a steady rhythm and then purposely disrupting that pattern by accenting beats where they are not expected.

Like jazz ensembles, learning organizations also intentionally create a sense of disequilibrium. Dissonance is established by exploiting the contention between opposing points of view, especially the clash between external demands for change and internal tendencies toward stability. Syncopation is created by purposely disrupting habitual patterns as a means of promoting change. Without dissonance and syncopation, prevailing mind-sets become entrenched, and organizations lose their capacity to anticipate and respond to change in the business environment.

A Learning Community

Finally, members of jazz ensembles recognize that, above all else, they belong to a community of people learning collectively and collaboratively together. It is not the great soloist that produces great jazz, but the combined expression of the ensemble. "As the musicians feel the direction of the music that is developing out of their interwoven contributions," Schön (1983) observes, "they make new sense of it and adjust their performance to the new sense they have made. They are reflecting-in-action on the music they are collectively making and on their individual contributions to it, thinking what they are doing and, in the process, evolving their way of doing it" (pp. 55–56).

Similarly, members of learning organizations recognize that they belong to a collaborative community. It is not the individual performance that determines how well and how fast a firm is able to learn and to change. It is the collective capability of a firm to create new knowledge, to deal with continuous and discontinuous change, and to learn from its own experiences that, more than anything else, will determine the degree to which it succeeds as a learning organization.

NOTES

Prologue

1. Arie de Geus's article, "Planning as Learning," is from *Harvard Business Review*, 1988, *66*(2), 70–74. Background on the petroleum industry and Royal Dutch/Shell's financial performance is excerpted from two articles: C. Loomis, "Dinosaurs?" *Fortune*, May 3, 1993, pp. 36–52; and C. Knowlton, "Shell Gets Rich at Beating Risk," *Fortune*, Aug. 26, 1991, pp. 79–84. The "management challenge" was reported by G. C. Hill and K. Yamada, "Staying Power: Motorola Illustrates How an Aging Giant Can Remain Vibrant," *Wall Street Journal*, December 9, 1992.

2. Interview with Alan Honeycutt, manager, Training and Organization Effectiveness, TRW Space and Defense Group.

3. Interview with Ramon A. Alvarez, vice president and general manager, Micro Switch Division, Honeywell.

4. This description is based on two sources: an interview with Deborah A. Lauer, director, Senior Executive Program Applications, Motorola; a presentation delivered by John Major, senior vice president and general manager of Worldwide Systems Group, Motorola, to the International Software Quality Exchange Conference, San Francisco, California, March 1992.

5. We are paraphrasing the words of Karl Weick ("Organization Design: Organizations as Self-Designing Systems," *Organization Dynamics*, 1977, *6*(2), p. 37), whose notion of "self-designing" organizations provided an early foundation for the later development of the notion of learning organizations.
6. Presentation by Eric Miller of the Tavistock Institute at Northwestern University, Chicago, Illinois, May 1992.

Chapter Three

1. Interview with Alan Honeycutt, manager, Training and Organization Effectiveness, TRW Space and Defense Group.

Chapter Four

1. From a speech delivered by John Major, senior vice president and general manager of Worldwide Systems Group, Motorola, to the International Software Quality Exchange Conference, San Francisco, California, March 1992.
2. This description of Southern California Edison's scenario planning process is from "Twelve Scenarios for Southern California Edison," *Planning Review*, 1992, *20*(3), 30-37.
3. This description is based on two sources: an interview with Deborah A. Lauer, director, Senior Executive Program Applications, Motorola; a presentation delivered by John Major, senior vice president and general manager of Worldwide Systems Group, Motorola, to the International Software Quality Exchange Conference, San Francisco, California, March 1992.
4. Interview with Alan Honeycutt, manager, Training and Organization Effectiveness, TRW Space and Defense Group.

Chapter Five

1. The General Products anecdote is from M. Beer, R. A. Eisenstadt, and B. Spector, *The Critical Path to Corporate Renewal* (Boston: Harvard Business School Press, 1990).
2. Described by Ray Stata in "Organizational Learning: The Key to Management Innovation," *Sloan Management Review*, Spring 1989, pp. 63-74.

3. Interview with Ramon A. Alvarez, vice president and general manager, Micro Switch Division, Honeywell.

Chapter Six

1. This description is based on two sources: an interview with Deborah A. Lauer, director, Senior Executive Program Applications, Motorola; a presentation delivered by John Major, senior vice president and general manager of Worldwide Systems Group, Motorola, to the International Software Quality Exchange Conference, San Francisco, California, March 1992.
2. This description is based on interviews with Thomas Broersma, as well as his doctoral dissertation "Organizational Learning and Aircrew Performance," University of Texas at Austin, 1992.
3. This example is drawn from I. Nonaka, "The Knowledge-Creating Company," *Harvard Business Review*, 1991, *69*(6), 96–104.
4. Interview with Ramon A. Alvarez, vice president and general manager, Micro Switch Division, Honeywell.

Chapter Seven

1. Interview with Ramon A. Alvarez, vice president and general manager, Micro Switch Division, Honeywell.
2. From *Blueprints for Service Quality: The Federal Express Approach*, AMA management briefing (New York: American Management Association, 1991). Also, P. Galagan, "Training Delivers Results to Federal Express," *Training and Development Journal*, 1991, *45*(12), 27–33.
3. Background on General Motors is from two articles: A. Taylor, "What's Ahead for GM's New Team," *Fortune*, 1992, *126*(12), 58–61; and C. Loomis, "Dinosaurs?" *Fortune*, May 3, 1993, pp. 36–52. The description of inquiry centers is from V. P. Barabba and G. Zaltman, "The Inquiry Center," *Planning Review*, 1991, *19*(2), 4–9, 47–48.
4. Interview with Ramon A. Alvarez, vice president and general manager, Micro Switch Division, Honeywell.
5. This description of the work of The Consortium for Produc-

tivity in the Schools is based upon interviews with and documents provided by Sue Berryman, chair of the Consortium, Steve Goldman, director of the Ball Foundation, its sponsor, and Jennifer Kemeny and Sherry Immediato of Innovation Associates.

Chapter Eight

1. This description of College Pro Painters was based on interviews with Paul Woolner of Woolner, Lowy & Associates, a consultant to College Pro Painters.
2. This description is based upon P. Woolner, "Integrated Work and Learning: A Developmental Model of the Learning Organization," an unpublished paper presented at the annual conference of the Commission of Professors of Adult Education, Montreal, Canada, 1991, as well as interviews with the author.
3. Interview with Mark Cheren, president, Strategic Learning Services.
4. Shell's "management challenge" is described in M. Pedler, J. Burgoyne, and T. Boydell, *The Learning Company: A Strategy for Sustainable Development* (New York: McGraw-Hill, 1991), p. 54.
5. From G. C. Hill and K. Yamada, "Staying Power: Motorola Illustrates How an Aging Giant Can Remain Vibrant," *Wall Street Journal*, December 9, 1992.
6. From A. Lewis and W. Marsh, "Action Learning: The Development of Field Managers in the Prudential Assurance Company," *Journal of Management Development*, 1987, *6*(2), 45–56.
7. From J. L. Noel and R. Charan, "GE Brings Global Thinking to Light," *Training and Development Journal*, 1992, *46*(7), 29–33.
8. From Udai Pareek, "Organizational Learning Diagnostics (OLD): Assessing and Developing Organizational Learning," in *The 1988 Annual: Developing Human Resources*, San Diego: Pfeiffer & Company, 1988, 125–135.
9. This study was conducted by several leading researchers in the

field of learning organizations, including Ralph Catalanello, Nancy Dixon, Victoria Marsick, Judy O'Neil, and Karen Watkins. Preliminary results were presented at the National Conference of the American Society for Training and Development, Atlanta, Georgia, May 1993.

10. For information on *The Learning Organization Profile,* contact Dr. Michael J. O'Brien, O'Brien Learning Systems, 949 Woodcreek Drive, Milford, Ohio 45150.

Chapter Nine

1. The discussion of the Tavistock Institute, sociotechnical redesign, and self-organizing systems is based upon publications of members of the Tavistock Institute: F. E. Emery and E. L. Trist, *Towards a Social Ecology* (New York: Plenum, 1973); and E. L. Trist, G. W. Higgin, H. Murray, and A. B. Pollock, *Organizational Choice* (London: Tavistock, 1963). We also rely upon excellent summarizations provided by both G. Morgan, *Images of Organization* (Newbury Park, Calif.: Sage, 1986); and M. Weisbord, *Productive Workplaces: Organizing and Managing for Dignity, Meaning, and Community* (San Francisco: Jossey-Bass, 1987).

2. This description of Hanover Insurance is from C. Hampden-Turner, "Charting the Dilemmas of Hanover Insurance," *Planning Review,* 1992, *20*(1), 22–28; and from C. Hampden-Turner, *Charting the Corporate Mind* (New York: Free Press, 1990).

Epilogue

1. A similar assertion was made by A. P. de Geus, "Planning as Learning," *Harvard Business Review,* 1988, *66*(2), 70–74. Bob Garratt offered an equation (rate of learning $\geq$ rate of change = survival) to capture Reg Revans's idea that the rate of learning in organizations must be equal to or greater than the rate of change in environments for firms to survive ("The Power of Action Learning," in M. Pedler (ed.), *Action Learning in Practice.* Aldershot, Hants, England: Gower, 1992). We combined these two ideas to create the equation presented here.

2. We would like to think that we were the only people to see the metaphoric link between jazz improvisation and learning organizations. But we were not. Others include Lee Tom Perry, "Strategic Improvising: How to Formulate and Implement Competitive Strategies in Concert," *Organizational Dynamics,* Spring 1991, pp. 51–64; Peter Senge, *The Fifth Discipline* (New York: Doubleday, 1990); and Donald Schön, *The Reflective Practitioner* (New York: Basic Books, 1983).

REFERENCES

Argyris, C. "Strategy Implementation: An Experience in Learning." *Organizational Dynamics*, 1989, *18*(2), 5–15.

Argyris, C., and Schön, D. *Organizational Learning: A Theory of Action Perspective*. Reading, Mass.: Addison-Wesley, 1978.

Ashby, W. R. *Design for a Brain*. London: Chapman and Hall, 1952.

Baburoglu, O., and Garr, M. A. "Search Conference Methodology for Practitioners." In M. Weisbord (ed.), *Discovering Common Ground*. San Francisco: Berrett-Koehler, 1992.

Barabba, V. P., and Zaltman, G. "The Inquiry Center." *Planning Review*, 1991, *19*(2), 4–9, 47–48.

Beer, M., Eisenstat, R. A., and Spector, B. *The Critical Path to Corporate Renewal*. Boston: Harvard Business School Press, 1990.

Blueprints for Service Quality: The Federal Express Approach. AMA management briefing. New York: American Management Association, 1991.

Bolman, L. G., and Deal, T. E. *Reframing Organizations: Artistry, Choice, and Leadership*. San Francisco: Jossey-Bass, 1991.

Broersma, T. J. "Organizational Learning and Aircrew Performance." Unpublished doctoral dissertation, University of Texas at Austin, 1992.

Burns, T., and Stalker, G. M. *The Management of Innovation.* London: Tavistock Institute, 1961.

Carnall, C. "Managing Strategic Change: An Integrated Approach." *Long-Range Planning,* 1986, *19*(6), 105-115.

"A Conversation with Robert W. Galvin." Interviewed by Kenneth R. Thompson. *Organizational Dynamics,* 1992, *20*, 56-69.

Davidow, W. H., and Malone, M. S. *The Virtual Corporation.* New York: Harper Business, 1992.

de Geus, A. P. "Planning as Learning." *Harvard Business Review,* 1988, *66*(2), 70-74.

Drucker, P. "The New Society of Organizations." *Harvard Business Review,* 1992, *70*(5), 95-104.

Emery, F. E., and Trist, E. L. "Socio-Technical Systems." In C. W. Churchman and others (eds.), *Management Sciences: Models and Techniques:* London: Pergamon Press, 1960.

Emery, F. E., and Trist, E. L. *Towards a Social Ecology.* New York: Plenum, 1973.

Galagan, P. "Training Delivers Results to Federal Express." *Training and Development Journal,* 1991, *45*(12), 27-33.

Garratt, B. "The Power of Action Learning." In M. Pedler (ed.), *Action Learning in Practice.* Aldershot, Hants, England: Gower, 1992.

Garvin, D. "How the Baldrige Award Really Works." *Harvard Business Review,* 1991, *69*(6), 80-95.

Garvin, D. "Building a Learning Organization." *Harvard Business Review,* 1993, *71*(4), 78-91.

Hammer, M. "Reengineering Work: Don't Automate, Obliterate." *Harvard Business Review,* 1990, *68*(4), 104-112.

Hampden-Turner, C. *Charting the Corporate Mind.* New York: Free Press, 1990.

Hampden-Turner, C. "Charting the Dilemmas of Hanover Insurance." *Planning Review,* 1992, *20*(1), 22-28.

Handy, C. *The Age of Unreason.* Boston: Harvard Business School Press, 1990.

Henkoff, R. "How to Plan for 1995." *Fortune,* 1990, *122*(16), 70-79.

Hicks, J. P. "The Steel Man with Kid Gloves." *New York Times,* Apr. 3, 1992, p. C-1.

Hill, G. C., and Yamada, K. "Staying Power: Motorola Illustrates

How an Aged Giant Can Remain Vibrant." *Wall Street Journal,* Dec. 9, 1992.

Kanter, R. M. *When Giants Learn to Dance.* New York: Simon and Schuster, 1989.

Kanter, R. M. "Change: Where to Begin." *Harvard Business Review,* 1991, *69*(4), 8–9.

Kiechel, W. "The Organization That Learns." *Fortune,* Mar. 12, 1990, pp. 133–136.

Knowlton, C. "Shell Gets Rich at Beating Risk." *Fortune,* Aug. 26, 1991, pp. 79–84.

Kolb, D. A. *Experiential Learning.* Englewood Cliffs, N.J.: Prentice-Hall, 1984.

Kuhn, T. S. *The Structure of Scientific Revolutions.* (2nd ed.) Chicago: University of Chicago Press, 1970.

Lessem, R. *Total Quality Learning: Building a Learning Organization.* Oxford, England: Basil Blackwell, 1991.

Lewin, K. *Field Theory in Social Science.* New York: HarperCollins, 1951.

Lewis, A., and Marsh, W., "Action Learning: The Development of Field Managers in the Prudential Assurance Company." *Journal of Management Development,* 1987, *6*(2), 45–56.

Loomis, C. "Dinosaurs?" *Fortune,* May 3, 1993, pp. 36–52.

Major, J. "Providing the Software Solution: Motorola's Experiment in Cultural Transformation." Speech delivered to International Software Quality Exchange Conference, San Francisco, March 1992.

Marsick, V., Cederholm, L., Turner, E., and Pearson, T. "Action Reflection Learning." *Training and Development Journal,* 1992, *46*(8), 63–66.

Michaels, M. "The Neuralnet Organization: Part II." *Chaos Newsletter,* 1991, *3*(4), 1–4.

Miller, E. J. *The "Leicester" Model: Experiential Study of Group and Organizational Processes.* London: Tavistock Institute of Human Relations, 1989.

Mintzberg, H., and Waters, J. A. "Of Strategies, Deliberate and Emergent." *Strategic Management Journal,* 1985, *6*, 257–272.

Mohrman, S. A., and Cummings, T. G. *Self-Designing Organizations.* Reading, Mass.: Addison-Wesley, 1989.

Morgan. G. *Images of Organization.* Newbury Park, Calif.: Sage, 1986.

Morgan, G., and Ramirez, R. "Action Learning: A Holographic Metaphor for Guiding Social Change." *Human Relations,* 1984, *37*(1), 1-27.

Noel, J. L., and Charan, R. "GE Brings Global Thinking to Light." *Training and Development Journal,* 1992, *46*(7), 29-33.

Nonaka, I. "The Knowledge-Creating Company." *Harvard Business Review,* 1991, *69*(6), 96-104.

Normann, R. "Developing Capabilities for Organizational Learning." In J. Pennings and Associates (eds.), *Organizational Strategy and Change.* San Francisco: Jossey-Bass, 1985.

O'Brien, M. *The Learning Organization Profile.* Milford, Ohio: O'Brien Learning Systems, 1993.

Ostranski, L. *The Anatomy of Jazz.* Seattle, Wash.: University of Washington Press, 1973.

"Pan American World Airways: 1927-1991." *Newsweek,* July 22, 1991, p. 36.

Pareek, U. "Organizational Learning Diagnostics (OLD): Assessing and Developing Organizational Learning." In *The 1988 Annual: Developing Human Resources.* San Diego: Pfeiffer & Co., 1988.

Pascale, R. *Managing on the Edge: How the Smartest Companies Use Conflict to Stay Ahead.* New York: Simon and Schuster, 1990.

Pedler, M. *Action Learning in Practice.* Aldershot, Hants, England: Gower, 1992.

Pedler, M., Burgoyne, J., and Boydell, T. *The Learning Company: A Strategy for Sustainable Development.* New York: McGraw-Hill, 1991.

Perry, L. T. "Strategic Improvising: How to Formulate and Implement Competitive Strategies in Concert." *Organizational Dynamics,* Spring, 1991, pp. 51-64.

Peters, T. *Liberation Management.* New York: Knopf, 1992.

Pfeiffer, J. W., and Jones, J. E. "OD Readiness." In J. W. Pfeiffer and J. E. Jones (eds.), *The 1978 Annual Handbook for Group Facilitators.* La Jolla, Calif.: University Associates, 1978.

Prahalad, C. K., and Hamel, G. "The Core Competence of the Corporation." *Harvard Business Review,* 1990, *68*(3), 79-81.

Redding, J. "An Analysis of Three Strategic Training Roles: Their Impact upon Strategic Planning Problems." Unpublished doctoral dissertation, Northern Illinois University, 1990.

Reimann, B. C., and Ramanujam, V. "Acting Versus Thinking: A Debate Between Tom Peters and Michael Porter." *Planning Review*, 1992, *20*(2), 36–43.

Revans, R. W. *The Origins and Growth of Action Learning*. Chartwell/Brant, England: Bromley, 1982.

Revans, R. W. "Action Learning: Its Origins and Nature." In M. Pedler (ed.), *Action Learning in Practice*. Aldershot, Hants, England: Gower, 1991.

Savage, C. *Fifth Generation Management*. Maynard, Mass.: Digital Press, 1990.

Schein, E. H. "How Can Organizations Learn Faster? The Challenge of Entering the Green Room." *Sloan Management Review*, Spring 1993, pp. 85–92.

Schön, D. *The Reflective Practitioner*. New York: Basic Books, 1983.

Schwartz, P. *The Art of the Long View*. New York: Doubleday, 1991.

Senge, P. *The Fifth Discipline*. New York: Doubleday, 1990.

Senge, P. "The Learning Organization Made Plain." *Training and Development Journal*, 1991, *45*(10), 37–44.

Simon, H. A. *The Science of the Artificial*. Cambridge, Mass.: MIT Press, 1969.

Stacey, R. D. *Managing the Unknowable: Strategic Boundaries Between Order and Chaos in Organizations*. San Francisco: Jossey-Bass, 1992.

Stata, R. "Organizational Learning: The Key to Management Innovation." *Sloan Management Review*, Spring 1989, pp. 63–74.

Steinberg, C. "Taking Charge of Change." *Training and Development Journal*, 1992, *46*(3), 26–32.

Stern, R. L. "The End of an Empire." *Forbes*, 1991, *147*(3), 74–76.

Taylor, A. "What's Ahead for GM's New Team." *Fortune*, 1992, *126*(12), 58–61.

Tenaglia, M., and Noonan, P. "Scenario-Based Strategic Planning: A Process for Building Top Management Consensus." *Planning Review*, 1992, *20*(2), 12–19.

Trist, E. L., Higgin, G. W., Murray, H., and Pollock, A. B. *Organizational Choice.* London: Tavistock Institute, 1963.

"Twelve Scenarios for Southern California Edison." *Planning Review, 20*(3), 30–37.

Ulrich, D., and Lake, D. *Organizational Capability.* New York: Wiley, 1990.

Vaill, P. B. *Managing as a Performing Art: New Ideas for a World of Chaotic Change.* San Francisco: Jossey-Bass, 1989.

Waterman, R. H. *The Renewal Factor.* New York: Bantam, 1987.

Waterman, R. H. *Adhocracy: The Power to Change.* Knoxville, Tenn.: Whittle, 1990.

Weick, K. E. "Organization Design: Organizations as Self-Designing Systems." *Organization Dynamics,* 1977, *6*(2), 30–46.

Weisbord, M. *Productive Workplaces: Organizing and Managing for Dignity, Meaning, and Community.* San Francisco: Jossey-Bass, 1987.

Weisbord, M. *Discovering Common Ground.* San Francisco: Berrett-Koehler, 1992.

Wheatley, M. *Leadership and the New Science.* San Francisco: Berrett-Koehler, 1992.

Woolner, P. "Integrated Work and Learning: A Developmental Model of the Learning Organization." Unpublished paper presented at the annual conference of the Commission of Professors of Adult Education, Montreal, Can., 1991.

Woolner, P., and Lowy, A. "A Developmental Model of the Learning Organization." Paper presented to the Chicago chapter of the American Society for Training and Development, Chicago, 1993.

Zenger, J. "How Do You Really Change an Organization?" Unpublished paper, Cupertino, Calif.: Zenger-Miller, 1988.

INDEX

193